在帕德拉奇生病期间,这个孤独的老人和快乐的小孩逐渐对他产生了感情。

有时候,在安特卫普的大街上,某位主妇会给他们端来一碗汤和一些面包。

然而孩子的心无时无刻不在强烈地渴望,渴望能够看到那两幅被遮盖起来的伟大的鲁本斯的巨作。

那天,牧草地里的再生草刚刚被割掉。

整个春、夏、秋三季,尼洛都在画这幅珍贵的作品。

他经过磨坊屋的时候已经是夜晚了。他认识阿洛伊斯房间那扇小窗子。

原先那里的人们对他们都是笑脸相迎,快乐地打招呼,而现在这些人都低着头,眼睛朝下,说话也只是只言片语。

雪下得很紧,飓风从北面猛烈刮来,平原上冷得要死。

这一天，很快又过了些时候，一位世界著名的画家也来到了这里。

他们终生相守在一起，死后也没有分离。

鲁本斯的故乡,故事就发生在这样一个地方。

鲁本斯作品:《升起十字架》,1610—1611年。

鲁本斯作品:《基督下十字架》,1611—1614年。

鲁本斯作品:《圣母升天图》,1626年。

佛兰德斯的狗
A Dog Of Flanders

[英] 奥维达 著
王家湘 译

北京出版集团
北京十月文艺出版社

正餐前的开胃小菜

王家湘

这本小书是19世纪英国女作家奥维达（1839—1908）在1872年出版的。她原名叫玛丽·路易斯·德拉雷米，幼小时把自己的名字说成了"奥维达"，后来就把奥维达用作了笔名。二十岁时第一次给杂志写故事，一生出版了四十五部作品，多数以上流社会生活为背景，流行一时后便逐渐被淡忘。1871年，奥维达到安特卫普游览，深为这座城市和鲁本斯的画作所打动，于1872年出版了《佛兰德斯的狗》，这个少年和忠狗的故事至今仍受到读者的喜爱，并在全世界广为流传，被翻译成多种文字，在美国被四次拍成电影，在日本被改编成动画片。在尼洛的故乡霍布肯小城，人们还在1985年为他和忠狗帕德拉奇建造了一座雕像。奥维达的这个故事吸引了来自四面八方的游人，他们都想亲眼看一看尼洛的故乡，看一看他钟爱的安特卫普市和市内的安特卫普大教堂。

故事所发生的时代离现在已经整整一百四十年了。佛兰德斯原是中世纪的一个公国，在今天的低地国家——荷兰、比利时、卢森堡——西南部。佛兰德斯公国于9世纪中叶开始扩张，到11世纪末已经深入法国领土。12世纪初，法国入侵并统治了佛兰德斯。在15世纪至17世纪的时候，佛兰德斯为西班牙所统治，在法国革命过程中，佛兰德斯已经不再是一个政治实体。现在的佛兰德斯是一个地理概念，包括法国的北部省、比利时的东佛兰德斯省和西佛兰德斯省以及荷兰的泽兰省。

尼洛和帕德拉奇的家在比利时，是一个离安特卫普市三英里的叫霍布肯的小村庄，他们每天都要用小车把牛奶拉到安特卫普市去卖。在尼洛生活的时代，安特卫普市内街道狭窄弯曲，建筑陈旧，这在故事里都有十分真实的描述。但是，安特卫普是佛兰德斯最著名的画家鲁本斯画下了他最著名的作品的城市，正是鲁本斯的杰作催生了少年尼洛的艺术之梦，拥有鲁本斯巨作的安特卫普大教堂成了尼洛膜拜之地，也是他和帕德拉奇离开这个"爱心得不到报答、信念没办法实现的世界"的地方。

建造安特卫普大教堂，前后一共用了一百七十年时间（1351—1521）。大教堂的钟楼尖顶高一百二十三米，钟楼里有一组由四十七口大钟组成的排钟，尼洛在家门口就能够望见远处高耸的教堂钟楼尖顶，从中得到支持他实现梦想的力量。今天，在安特卫普大教堂里，悬挂着鲁本斯的三幅著名作品，当年激发了尼洛对艺术强烈激情的《圣母升天图》[①]，是鲁本斯用了十五年时间，为安特卫普大教堂于1626年完成的。而尼洛梦寐以求、希望能够看上一眼的另外两幅作品，一幅是在1610年至1611年间画家为圣沃博加教堂创作的祭坛画《升起十字架》[②]；另一幅是在1611年至1614年为安特卫普大教堂创作的祭坛画《基督下十字架》[③]。

---

①②③　译法参照《简明不列颠百科全书》。

这两幅画，尼洛因为贫困而无缘一睹，直到离开这个世界之前，才在清冷的月光下得以看上一眼。

现在，北京十月文艺出版社要出版这个故事的对照阅读版，译者希望译文能够对喜爱文学和希望提高英语阅读鉴赏能力的读者有一点帮助。我毕生从事英语语言文学的教学工作，近三十余年也翻译了一些英美作家的文学作品，作为教师和翻译者，我特别重视对原文的正确理解，出于对原作者和读者的尊重，我在翻译中从来不删改原文。这是其一。其二是，我认为作家和作品的风格是阅读欣赏，甚至是理解作品的重要一环，我会尽可能在翻译过程中注意作品风格上的特点，原文简约或是华丽、直白或是隐晦、流畅或是晦涩，译文就要尽量有所反映。所以，译文的汉语风格其实不应该是译者自己写作时的风格，而应该是所译作品的作者的风格。

世界上任何一种使用中的语言，都会随着时代的发展变化而发展变化。奥维达的作品写于一百四十年前，在中国是清朝的同治时代。试想如果阅读那个时期的文章，现代人很多都读不懂了。奥维达时代的英语和现代英语之间的差别，没有现代汉语和同治时期汉语之间的差别大，但是许多词语的用法和意义都有一定的发展和变化，句子结构较为复杂，可能会给今天的中国读者带来一些不便。如果进行两种语言间的对照阅读，可能会给读者一定的帮助。

译文依据的是美国www.ReadHowYouWant.com出版的2006年版。全书分为十四章，我们认为这个版本的分章比较好，就按它将译文分为十四章。其中第五章的第四、第五两段，我们根据故事情节，依照其他版本调整了顺序。究竟初版时故事是怎么分章的，已难以查考了。好在这个版本与其他版本相比，文字上的出入极少，所以是可以信赖的。

开胃菜吃了，下面可以用正餐了。希望你们喜欢。

目 录

第一章 …………………………… 1

第二章 …………………………… 5

第三章 …………………………… 11

第四章 …………………………… 16

第五章 …………………………… 21

第六章 …………………………… 27

第七章 …………………………… 33

第八章 …………………………… 39

第九章 …………………………… 45

第十章 …………………………… 49

第十一章 ………………………… 56

第十二章 ………………………… 62

第十三章 ………………………… 67

第十四章 ………………………… 74

附录:《佛兰德斯的狗》英文原著 …… 77

第一章

尼洛和帕德拉奇被孤苦伶仃地留在了世界上。

他们是朋友,他们的友谊胜过亲兄弟。尼洛是一个小小的阿登高地①人;帕德拉奇是一只大大的佛拉芒②狗。他们年龄相同,但是一个仍然年轻,另一个已经老了。他们几乎一直生活在一起:他们都是孤儿,一贫如洗,是同一双手使他们活了下来。他们之间的亲密关系是从最初的相互同情开始的。岁月日益加深了这个关

---

① 阿登高地:西欧的一个地区,包括比利时的东、西佛兰德斯省,卢森堡南部和法国东北部地区。
② 佛拉芒:原指佛拉芒人,为原住东、西佛兰德斯省的比利时两个民族之一。

系，和他们一同成长，成为坚不可摧的力量，使他们彼此深深相爱。

他们的家是个小屋子，在一个小村边上。这是个佛拉芒人的村落，离安特卫普市三英里，四周是宽阔平展的牧场和玉米地，大运河穿流而过，沿岸一行行长长的杨树和桤树在微风中摇曳。小村里有二十来所房屋和带土地的宅院，都有鲜绿或天蓝色的百叶窗，玫瑰红或黑白相间的屋顶，以及粉刷得犹如白雪、在阳光下闪闪发光的墙壁。

村子中心耸立着一座风车磨坊，建在一片长满青苔的坡地上，是周围平坦的乡村地区的一个地标性建筑。它一度被漆成鲜红色，包括翼板等等在内，但那是半个多世纪以前、建成不久时候的事了，那时它为拿破仑的士兵磨过麦子。如今，在常年的风吹日晒之下，它已经变成了红褐色。风车行为古怪，转转停停，仿佛年纪大了，得了风湿病，关节僵硬，但是它仍在为周边所有的居民服务。他们会认为把谷物拿到别处去磨，是极不虔诚的行为，简直就像到别的教堂去做礼拜，而不是去到那座古老的、小小的灰色教堂的圣坛前做弥撒一样。这座有着圆锥形尖顶的灰色教堂就在风车磨坊对面,每天早晨、中午和晚上,教堂那口唯一的钟便会敲响,它的钟声如同悬挂在低地国家①的每一口钟的声音一样,带着独特的抑郁和低沉的哀伤,似乎成了其旋律中不可或缺的一部分。

尼洛和帕德拉奇几乎从一出生起,就在这忧郁的钟声中一同生活在村边这所小屋里。在小屋的东北方,越过像风平浪静、亘古不变的大海般伸展开去的,种植着牧草和玉米的巨大的绿色平原,高耸着安特卫普大教堂的尖顶。小屋的主人叫杰汉·达斯,是一个又老又穷的老头子。他年轻时当过兵,还记得那些如牛群踏平耕地般蹂躏国土的战争。当兵只给他留下了创伤,使他成了个跛子。

老杰汉·达斯八十岁那年,他的女儿在阿登高地的斯塔夫罗特附近去世了,给他留下了一个两岁大的儿子。老人连自己都养活不了,但还是毫无怨言地挑起了这额外的担子。很快,孩子得到他的欢心,成了他的宝

---

① 低地国家:指西欧的荷兰、比利时、卢森堡三国。

贝。尼洛的大名叫尼古拉斯，尼洛是爱称。小尼洛和老人在一起，茁壮地成长起来，一老一小心满意足地居住在那个贫困的小屋里。

确实，那是座非常简陋的小泥屋，但却像贝壳一样洁白干净。屋外是一片小菜园，生长着豆类、各种香草和南瓜。他们很穷，真的穷极了——在许多日子里，他们根本没有东西吃。他们从来没有吃饱过；吃顿饱饭等于一下子就进了天堂。但老人对孩子非常温柔慈祥，小孩也天真漂亮、诚实、心地善良。能有一块干面包和几片菜叶子吃，他们就会很开心，不再向天地上苍有什么别的要求，只要帕德拉奇永远和他们在一起就行，因为没有帕德拉奇，哪里会有他们呢？

帕德拉奇是他们的一切：他们的宝库和粮仓，他们的黄金储藏和财富魔杖，养家糊口的力量和精神支柱，唯一的朋友和慰藉。如果帕德拉奇死去或离开他们，他们也必定会倒下死去。帕德拉奇是他们俩的躯体、大脑，他们的头和四肢；帕德拉奇就是他们的生命，他们的灵魂。因为杰汉·达斯老了，腿又瘸，尼洛还只是个小孩子；而帕德拉奇是他们的狗。

第二章

佛兰德斯狗有黄色的皮毛,头和四肢很大,耳朵像狼耳,总是直立着,腿呈弓形,脚掌宽大,是这个种群世代干苦活因而肌肉发达的结果。帕德拉奇来自一个辛劳苦干的家族,许多世纪以来,佛兰德斯老百姓家用的狗都出自这个家族,他们一代又一代备受奴役,驾辕拉车,活着的时候在苦难的拉车生涯中耗尽精力,最后倒在街道的硬石上心脏破裂而死。

帕德拉奇的爹妈劳苦终身,奔波在各个城市石铺的道路上,奔波在两个佛兰德斯省和布拉邦特的无遮无拦、令人厌倦的漫长大路上。痛苦和辛劳是他唯一的继承。他在辱骂中长大，拳脚相加是他的洗礼。有什么不可以的呢？这是个笃信基督教的国家，而帕德拉奇只不过是条狗而已。他还没有成年就已经饱尝肩拉颈缚之苦。出生不到十三个月，就成了一个五金商人的财产。商人习惯于南北闯荡，从蔚蓝的大海到碧绿的群山。原来的主人很便宜就把他卖给了这个人，因为他只有那么小。

这家伙是个酒鬼加畜生。帕德拉奇过着地狱般的生活。将地狱的酷刑施加在动物身上，是基督徒用来表现他们对基督教的信仰的一种方式。帕德拉奇的买主是个阴郁、粗暴、凶残的布拉邦特人，他把车子装满了锅碗瓢盆、酒壶水桶，以及其他各种陶器、铜器和锡器，听任帕德拉奇拼命地拉车，而他自己则在一旁悠闲地走着，懒洋洋地无比自在，叼着黑烟斗吸烟，一路上遇到酒馆或咖啡店都要进去光顾一番。

对于帕德拉奇来说，幸运或者说不幸的是，他来自一个有铁打的身板的族类，非常健壮，生来就习惯了这种无比沉重的劳动，所以他没有死去，而是在残酷的压迫下悲惨地活了下来。佛拉芒人给他们最吃苦耐劳的四脚受害者的唯一报酬就是：用鞭子抽破他们的皮肉、饥饿干渴、痛打、咒骂，无休止地干活，直到筋疲力尽为止。

就这样过了漫长而极其痛苦的两年。一天，帕德拉奇和往常一样，正行走在一条通往鲁本斯之城①的大路上。这是一条尘土飞扬、毫无可爱之处的笔直大路。当时正是炎热的盛夏时光，他拉的车十分沉重，堆满了高高的金属制品和陶器。主人悠然自得地走着，除了抽动鞭子打在他颤抖的脊背上之外，并没有注意到他。这个布拉邦特人在每一家路边酒馆都要停下来喝啤酒，但是却不许帕德拉奇停下片刻去沟渠边喝口水。他就这样在太阳的暴晒下，行走在灼热的大路上。他已经二十四个小时没有吃过任何东西了，更糟的是，几乎十二个小时滴水未沾。尘土蒙住了他的眼睛，鞭子抽打得他浑身疼痛，腰背上的无情重负使他麻木，帕德拉奇摇晃了几下，口吐白沫，倒在了地上。

他倒在白色的满是尘土的大路中间，倒在毒辣的阳

---

① 鲁本斯（1577—1640）：佛兰德斯著名画家，此处"鲁本斯之城"指鲁本斯生活与成长的城市安特卫普。

光下,一动不动,病得快要死了。他的主人给他的是自己药房里仅有的药——脚踢嘴骂、栎木棍打,其实这些经常就是帕德拉奇得到的唯一的吃喝,唯一的酬劳和回报。但是这时,帕德拉奇已经感觉不到任何的酷刑和咒骂了。他躺倒在炎夏白色的尘土里,看上去显然已经死了。过了一会儿,这个布拉邦特人发现,往他肋骨上打、往他耳朵里灌骂声全然不起任何作用,便认为帕德拉奇已经死了,或者差不多就要死了,尸体再也没有用了,除非有什么人会扒下他的皮来做手套。临走时,他恶狠狠地咒骂着帕德拉奇,扯下挽具上的皮带子,把他踢到一边的草丛里,然后怒冲冲地嘟囔着,有气无力地推着车子上坡而去,丢下奄奄一息的狗,任蚂蚁叮咬、乌鸦啄食。

明天就是一年一度的卢万城[①]守护神节[②]了,这位布

[①] 卢万城:比利时布拉邦特省城市。原是织布业中心。14世纪时是欧洲最大城市之一。不仅为主要的文化中心,也是一个农业市场。

[②] 守护神节 (kermesse):原是一个荷兰语词。最初指为纪念某教堂兴建周年并感谢赞助人举行的弥撒。庆典活动一般在低地国家及法国北部进行,伴有盛宴、舞蹈以及各种运动。

拉邦特人急着要赶去那里的集市，好为自己的一车铜制品占个有利于做买卖的好地方。他火冒三丈，帕德拉奇一向身强体壮，吃苦耐劳，而现在却要他自己辛辛苦苦地把车子一路推到卢万城去。但是，他根本就没有想到要留下来照看帕德拉奇，这畜生快死了，没有用了，他会去偷一条狗来代替帕德拉奇，去偷他看见的第一只独自溜达到主人视线以外的大狗。他没有在帕德拉奇身上花钱，或者说简直没花什么钱，而在漫长而残酷的两年里，他让帕德拉奇不停地为他从日出干到日落，无论酷暑严冬，天气好坏。

他已经充分使用了帕德拉奇，获得了很大的好处，因为他是人，他很聪明，便听任这狗独自在沟渠里咽下最后一口气，充血的眼睛很可能被鸟儿啄出，而他要继续赶路，在卢万城的欢乐气氛里去讨去偷、去吃去喝、去唱去跳。一条垂死的狗、拉车的狗，他为什么要冒损失一把铜币、被人嘲笑的风险，为他的痛苦挣扎浪费时间呢？

帕德拉奇被丢弃在草绿的沟渠里，一动不动地躺着。那天，这条路上人很多，成百的人或步行，或骑骡，或乘坐四轮或两轮马车经过这里，高高兴兴地赶往卢万城。有的人看见了帕德拉奇，多数人连瞧都没瞧，全都继续赶路。不过是条死狗而已，在布拉邦特，这不算什么事，在世界上任何地方都不算什么事。

第三章

过了一阵子,在过节的人群中出现了一个小老头,他驼着背,一瘸一瘸的,非常虚弱。他看上去不是去玩乐的,身上穿的衣服十分破烂,夹杂在寻欢作乐的人群中,一声不响,费劲而缓慢地走在满是尘土的大路上。他看了看帕德拉奇,停下脚步,觉得有点奇怪,转身跪在了沟渠旁丛生的杂草上,一双满怀同情的眼睛慈祥地查看着这只狗。有一个几岁大的小男孩和老人在一起,他面色红润,有金黄色的头发和黑色的眼睛。孩子"啪嗒啪嗒"地穿过齐胸高的灌木丛,然后站住,带着一副可爱的严肃神情,紧盯着这只可怜的、一动不动的大狗。

这就是他们俩——小小的尼洛和巨大的帕德拉奇的初次相遇。

那天，事情的结果是老杰汉·达斯费尽了力气，把遭难的狗拖回自己的小屋。小屋在田野上，离得不远，在那儿他精心护理病狗。帕德拉奇因酷热、干渴和疲劳而昏死过去，在阴凉处休息了一段时间以后，便苏醒过来，恢复了健康和体力，四条粗壮的黄褐色的腿又重新摇摇晃晃地站立了起来。

在许多个星期里，帕德拉奇都干不了活，没有力气，浑身酸痛，奄奄一息。但是却没有听到一句严苛的责骂，没有感到一次粗鲁的触摸，有的只是孩子喃喃的怜悯的声音，和老人给予他的满怀慰藉的抚爱。

在帕德拉奇生病期间，这个孤独的老人和快乐的小孩逐渐对他产生了感情。他在小屋里有了自己的一个角落，有了一张干草铺就的床，老人和孩子学会了在黑夜里焦急地留神倾听他的呼吸声，好知道他还活着。当他第一次恢复到能够大声发出一声低沉的吠叫时，他们大笑了起来，高兴得几乎一齐流下了眼泪，因为这表示他肯定已经痊愈了。小尼洛欢天喜地，把雏菊花环套在了他粗壮的脖子上，用清新红润的双唇亲吻他。

当帕德拉奇完全恢复，站立起来的时候，他巨大的身体有点消瘦，但强健有力，两只沉思的大眼睛里流露出一丝惊异的神情：没有催他醒来的责骂声，也没有逼他干活的殴打。于是，他心里焕发起一种强大的爱，只要他活着，对他们的忠心就从来没有动摇过。

作为一条狗，帕德拉奇懂得感恩。他躺在那里，久久地思索着，棕色的眼睛严肃地、深情地、沉思地注视着他朋友的一举一动。

这时，上了年纪的老兵杰汉·达斯没有别的谋生手段，只能每天推着一辆小车，一瘸一瘸地替比他幸运的、拥有奶牛的邻居们往安特卫普城送牛奶。村民们给他这个活干，部分是出于好心，更多是因为让这样诚实的一个人给他们送牛奶，对他们来说再合适不过了，他们自己可以留在家里照管菜园、奶牛、家禽，或者他们那一点田地。但是对于老人来说，这活儿变得越来越重了。他八十三岁了，而到安特卫普足足有三英里远，或许还不止呢。

恢复健康后的一天，帕德拉奇粗壮的脖子上挂着雏菊花环，躺在阳光下看着牛奶罐进进出出。

第二天早晨，在老人还没有来到小车跟前的时候，帕德拉奇站起身来，走向小车，站在小车的两个车把之间，就像表演哑剧，清楚地表示了他的愿望：他吃了他们施舍给他的面包，现在他有能力用工作来报答他们了。杰汉·达斯怎么也不肯答应，因为他认为，让狗干大自然没有赋予他们去干的苦力活是极其可耻的。但是帕德拉奇不容他反对，他发现他们不给他套挽具，便试图用牙拉着车往前走。

终于，杰汉·达斯让步了，这条他救活的狗的坚持和感激之情征服了他。他把小车改装了一下，好让帕德拉奇能够驾着车跑。从此，帕德拉奇每天早上都拉着车子去送奶。

冬天来临后，杰汉·达斯感谢自己的好运气把他在卢万城集市那天带到了沟渠里那条奄奄一息的狗的身边。他很老了，身体一年比一年虚弱，假如没有他救活的这条狗的勤奋和力气，他根本不知道怎样能够把装满牛奶罐的小车拉过雪地，拉过泥地上深深的车辙沟。

至于帕德拉奇，对他来说这就是天堂了。旧主人强迫他拉一车难以承受的重担，每走一步都有鞭子的催赶。现在，拉着这辆装着发亮的黄铜奶罐的轻快的绿色小车，走在和蔼的老人旁边，老人总是温柔地拍拍他、夸夸他，他觉得简直就像在玩乐一样。此外，三四点钟的时候活就干完了，然后他就可以干自己想干的事情了，比如说舒展自己的身子，躺在阳光下睡觉，在田野里四处溜达，和小家伙尼洛嬉戏，或者和别的狗朋友一起玩耍。帕德拉奇感到非常快乐。

对于他的平静生活来说，更为幸运的是，他的旧主人在梅赫伦[①]城的守护神节上醉酒打架，被打死了。因此不会再找他，更不会打搅他在深爱的新家的生活了。

---

① 梅赫伦：比利时安特卫普省的一个城市，那里的人说荷兰语。

第四章

几年以后,腿一直瘸着的老杰汉·达斯的风湿病愈加严重,使他行动困难,已经不可能再跟着小车去送奶了。这时,小尼洛已经长到六岁,他多次跟着外公去安特卫普,因此对这座城市非常熟悉,便接过了老人的位置,跟在小车旁边卖牛奶,收钱,然后把钱带回来,一本正经地有礼貌地交给牛奶的主人,他可爱的样子让所有看见他的人都非常喜欢他。

这个小小的阿登高地人是个漂亮孩子,有双温柔而严肃的黑眼睛,红润可爱的脸蛋,金色的头发围绕在脖子旁。尼洛和帕德拉奇经过的时候,许多画家都会给他们画上一幅速写：一辆载着泰尼耶家、米里斯家、范塔尔家的黄铜奶罐的绿色小车，一条黄褐色的结实的大狗，一走起来挽具上的铃铛就会发出快乐的叮咚声，以及跟着大狗奔跑的小人儿，白白的小脚上穿着一双大木鞋，柔嫩、严肃的脸上一副天真、快乐的神情，就像鲁本斯画作中那些美丽可爱的孩子。

尼洛和帕德拉奇活儿干得这么出色，在一起又这么开心，所以夏天到来的时候，杰汉·达斯虽然身体好了一些，也不用再出门干活了，可以坐在家门口晒晒太阳，看着他们从菜园的小门离开，然后打个盹，做个梦，祈祷一番，钟敲三响的时候再醒过来，守候着等待他们回来。一回到家，帕德拉奇就会从挽具下挣脱出来，欢快地吠叫，尼洛会自豪地讲述当天做过的事情，然后他们就会一起走进屋子里去吃饭：吃黑面包，喝牛奶，也许是汤。他们会看到阴影在大平原上越拉越长，看到暮色逐渐遮盖了大教堂美丽的尖顶。然后他们就会一起躺下，老人做祈祷，他们俩就安宁地入睡。

日子就这样一天天、一年年地过去，尼洛和帕德拉奇生活得快乐、单纯而又健康。

春天和夏天是他们特别高兴的时候。佛兰德斯并不是一个讨人喜欢的地方，而鲁本斯的安特卫普城的四郊或许可以说是最不讨人喜欢的了。

玉米和油菜、牧场和耕地在这块毫无特点的平原上一片连着一片，单调地一再重复，十分乏味。除了某座荒凉的灰色钟楼和它一串串忧郁的钟声，或者某个穿过田间、背着稻谷捆的拾穗人或担着柴捆的樵夫的身影可以入画之外，一切都是千篇一律、毫无变化，没有丝毫的美景可言。住在山上或森林中的人来到这里会感到压抑，感到被禁锢在了那巨大沉闷的平原上单调无尽的伸展之中。

但平原是绿色的，非常富饶。它广阔的地平线虽然单调沉闷，却有着某种独特的魅力。河边蒲草丛中生长着野花，河岸上树木高大鲜亮。驳船从大树旁驶过时，阳光逆射下，巨大的船身一片黑色，驳船上小小的绿色桶子和彩旗在树叶衬托下显得分外鲜艳。

反正，对于一个孩子和一条狗来说，有绿色的植物和广阔的空间，就够得上是美景了。他们没有更高的要求，只要干完了活以后，能够躺在河边茂密的草丛里，看沉重的船只从身边驶过，把清新的带有咸味的大海的气息糅进乡间夏季的花香之中。

确实，冬天的日子要难过得多，天不亮就得冒着严寒起床，没有一天有足够的东西吃。在寒夜里，小屋比棚子也好不了多少，虽然在天气暖和的时候，小屋掩盖在一株巨大的攀藤下，看上去非常漂亮。不错，攀藤不会结出果实，但是从开花到秋收，它茂密的绿叶都会像花格窗一般覆盖着小屋。冬天的时候，寒风总能在破旧的小屋的墙壁上找到许多洞孔，而攀藤上的叶子都掉光了，黑沉沉的。屋外，光秃秃的田野显得十分凄凉萧索。有时候，屋内的地面会积水冻冰。冬天确实很艰难，尼洛白白的小胳膊小腿都被雪冻得麻木了，冰柱划破了帕德拉奇勇敢而不知疲倦的脚。

但是，即便如此，人们也从来没有听到过他们抱怨，孩子和狗谁也没有抱怨过。孩子的木鞋和狗的四条腿总在一起，勇敢地越过冰冻的田野，伴着挽具上小铃铛的叮咚声一路小跑。有时候，在安特卫普的大街上，某位主妇会给他们端来一碗汤和一些面包；有时候某个好心的商人，会在他们回家的路上，往他们的小车里放上些木柴；有时候他们自己村子里的某个妇人，也会让他们留下一些牛奶自己喝。然后，他们就会在薄暮中欢快地跑过白雪皑皑的土地，快乐地喊叫着冲进家门。

所以，总的说来，他们的生活还是不错的，相当不错。帕德拉奇在公路或者大街上遇见别的许多狗，见他们从天亮干到天黑，得到的只是打骂，拉完车时人们也是一脚把他们从车辕下踢开，听任他们挨饿受冻。看到这些，帕德拉奇心中十分感激自己的命运，认为这是这个世界上能够提供的最公平、最宽厚的命运了。虽然他确实在夜里经常饿着肚子躺下睡觉；虽然他不得不在夏天中午的酷热下和冬天黎明时刺骨的寒冷中干活；虽然他的脚常常被凹凸不平的人行道尖突的边缘划伤而疼痛；虽然他不得不完成超过他体力和违背他本性的任务；然而他仍然感激而且满足。他每天恪尽职守，他挚爱的人的眼睛赞许地对他微笑。对于帕德拉奇来说，这就足够了。

第五章

在帕德拉奇的生活中，只有一件事使他不安。事情是这样的。大家都知道，安特卫普城里到处都是年代久远的石头建筑，它们古老阴森，宏伟壮丽，耸立在弯曲的短巷里、挤在通道和酒店之间、高耸在水边，钟声响起在它们上空，从它们的拱门里不时传出阵阵响亮的音乐声。

这些昔日宏伟古老的圣殿依然在那里，被包围在贫穷肮脏之中，被包围在匆匆奔忙、拥挤的人群和丑恶之中，以及现代社会的商务交往之中。从早到晚，云朵在它们头顶飘过，鸟儿在它们四周盘旋，风儿在它们身旁呜咽。在它们脚下的土地里，安息着伟大的鲁本斯。

这位非凡的大师之伟大在安特卫普仍旧无所不在。在它狭窄的街道上，无论我们转向哪里，都浸透着他的光辉，一切卑微平庸的事物都因此而改观。当我们缓慢地行走在它弯曲的道路上、走过污浊的死水边、穿过臭气冲天的短巷的时候，他的精神与我们相伴，他具有史诗般的美的想象就在我们身边，曾经一度感受过他的脚步、留下过他的身影的石头建筑，似乎都起立用鲜活的声音谈论着他。对于我们来说，这座埋葬着鲁本斯的城市仍然通过他，而且仅仅通过他，活在我们的记忆中。

没有鲁本斯，安特卫普又算得了什么？一个肮脏、灰暗、喧闹的大卖场而已，除了在码头上做交易的商人之外，没有人会愿意看上它一眼的。有了鲁本斯，对全世界的人来说，安特卫普就是一个神圣的名字，是一片圣土，是伯利恒[①]，一位艺术之神诞生的地方；是各各

---

① 伯利恒：巴勒斯坦中部城镇，在耶路撒冷以南的朱地亚山区，传为耶稣基督之诞生地。

他①，一位艺术之神长眠的地方。

那座巨大的白色墓冢四周是如此肃静，这种肃静只有在响起管风琴的鸣奏声，以及唱诗班高唱《向圣母致敬》或《主啊，怜悯我们》时，才会被打破。在鲁本斯诞生地的中心，在圣雅克大教堂圣坛旁的高坛内的那座纯洁的大理石圣殿是他的丰碑，毫无疑问，没有任何别的艺术家拥有过更为伟大的丰碑了。

国人啊！你们应该无比珍视你们的伟大人物，因为只有通过他们，后人才会知道你们。佛兰德斯世世代代的人都十分明智。在鲁本斯生前，他们给予了这位最伟大的儿子以殊荣，死后仍极力光大他的名字。但是这种明智实在是并不多见了。

现在来说说帕德拉奇的苦恼。他们到安特卫普去的时候，小尼洛总会一次又一次地走进这些巨大、阴暗的石头建筑，它们宏伟而忧郁地高耸在一片拥挤的屋顶之上。孩子消失在它们黑暗的拱门里，而被留在外面人行道上的帕德拉奇，就会郁郁寡欢地、徒劳地寻思，究竟

---

① 各各他：传为耶稣蒙难、被钉死在十字架上的地方。

是什么样的魅力，会吸引他离开自己形影不离的、心爱的伙伴？有过一两次，他还真拉着牛奶车"哐啷哐啷"地走上台阶，试图亲自去看上一看，但总是立即被一个穿着黑衣服、挂着标识身份的银链子的高个子看门人挡了回去。帕德拉奇怕给小主人惹麻烦，只好断了这个念头，耐心地趴在教堂前，等着孩子重新出现。

使帕德拉奇不安的并不是尼洛走进这些石头建筑这件事，他知道人们都去教堂，村子里人人都到红色风车磨坊对面那座小小的、破败的灰色石头教堂里去。使他不安的是，小尼洛走出安特卫普的教堂时，神情总是怪怪的，脸色不是通红就是惨白，每次去过之后回到家里，他总是一声不吭地坐在那里呆呆地幻想，不想出去玩，只是凝视着河道远处暮色四合的天空，一副十分抑郁甚至可以说是忧伤的神情。

"究竟怎么了？"帕德拉奇十分纳闷。他觉得这个小家伙这么严肃，不会是件好事或自然的事，他只能以自己笨拙的方式，尽一切所能，无论是在洒满阳光的田野里，还是在热闹的集市上，把尼洛留在自己身边。但是尼洛去的不是一般的教堂，他最常去的是安特卫普大教堂，而帕德拉奇则被昆廷·马齐斯①大门的铁片挡在了外面的石头路上。他会伸伸腿脚、打哈欠叹气，甚至时不时地嗥叫上几声，但是这一切都起不了任何作用，直到大教堂关门的时候，孩子才不得不走出大门，用胳膊搂着狗的脖子，亲吻他宽阔的黄褐色额头，总是喃喃地说着同样的话："要是我能够看到它们就好了，帕德拉奇！——要是我能够看到它们就好了！"

"它们是什么东西呀？"帕德拉奇心里想道，一面用充满同情和渴望的大眼睛看着孩子。

有一天，当大教堂的守门人不在一旁、大门虚掩着的时候，他跟着他小小的朋友进去了一会儿，看到了"它们"：原来是在唱诗班席位两侧的两幅被遮盖着的巨画。

尼洛正跪在圣坛背壁装饰画《圣母升天图》之前，沉浸在痴迷之中。当他发现了帕德拉奇的时候，便站起身来，轻轻地把狗拉到室外。他脸上满是泪水，在经过

---

① 昆廷·马齐斯（Quetin Matsys, 1466—1529）：佛兰德斯画家，安特卫普画派奠基人之一。传说他当画家之前做过铁匠。他死去一百年后，在安特卫普大教堂正门立了一块浮雕的牌匾，上面刻着这样的话："曾经是名铁匠，后来是名画家。"

被遮盖的画幅时抬头看了看，对他的伙伴喃喃地说道："帕德拉奇，仅仅因为穷，给不起钱，就看不见画，实在是太可怕了！我敢肯定，他画这两幅画的时候，根本没有不让穷人看的意思。他会让我们随时看、天天看，这一点我敢肯定。而他们把美丽的画幅遮盖起来，遮盖在黑暗之中！它们不见天日，没有人观赏它们，除非有钱人来付了钱才能看到它们。要是我能看到它们，死了都愿意。"

可是，他看不到它们，帕德拉奇也帮不了他，因为想观赏《升起十字架》和《基督下十字架》这两幅壮丽的巨画，教堂要收一银币，而对尼洛和帕德拉奇来说，想要挣得一银币，就如同登上大教堂的尖顶一样，完全是他们力所不能及的事情。他们连一个子儿的富余钱都没有过，他们最多只能挣点钱够给炉子买一点木柴，使锅里有点汤。然而孩子的心无时无刻不在强烈地渴望，渴望能够看到那两幅被遮盖起来的伟大的鲁本斯的巨作。

第六章

　　这个阿登高地小人儿的整个灵魂,都被他对艺术一往情深的热爱所鼓舞激动。每天清晨,在太阳升起、人们走出家门之前,尼洛和一条大狗穿行在老城中,拉着牛奶车挨家挨户卖牛奶。他看上去只不过是个乡下小男孩,但此时他却生活在充满梦想的天堂里,这里的上帝是鲁本斯。尼洛又冷又饿,两只赤裸的脚上穿着木鞋,冬天的寒风吹乱了他的鬈发、掀起了他破旧的薄衣衫,而尼洛却深深陷入了沉思冥想之中,看到的只是《圣母升天图》中的圣母玛利亚美丽的面庞,金色的鬈发披在她的肩头,永恒的太阳的光辉照在她的额头上。在贫穷中生长、备受命运折磨、没有文化、没人在意的尼洛,却有着天赋的才能,这是对他的补偿还是祸害?

谁也不知道他具有的天赋,他自己和别人一样,也不知道。谁也不知道,知道的只有帕德拉奇,因为他们朝夕相伴。他看到他用粉笔在石头上画出各种各样的植物或者动物;听到他在他干草铺的小小床上,喃喃地向那位大师的灵魂哀婉胆怯地做出各种祈祷;留意到他的目光在夕阳西下时的晚霞中黯淡下来,或者他的面庞在黎明时升起的玫瑰色的朝霞中闪闪发光;他许许多多次感受到从年轻明亮的双眼中流下的热泪,滴落在自己满是皱褶的黄色额头上,那是混合了奇特的、无以名状的痛苦和欢乐的热泪。

"尼洛,如果我想到,当你长大成人以后,能够拥有这所小屋和这一小块地,给自己干活,邻居都称呼你'先生',我死了也心满意足了。"杰汉·达斯老人躺在床上,总是这样对尼洛说。拥有一小块土地、被小村里的人称作先生,就是实现了一个佛拉芒农夫的最高理想;而这位老兵,年轻时走遍世界,但是什么也没有带回来，老了以后，他认为，能够在同一个地方谦卑而满足地生活和死去，是他能为心爱的外孙企望的最好的命运。但是尼洛什么话也没有说。

在过去的时代，艺术的酵母曾经催生了鲁本斯、约尔丹斯①、凡·艾克兄弟②，以及所有像他们一样卓越的群体，最近这几年来，在阿登高地的绿色乡间，在默兹河③水冲刷第戎④古老城墙的地方，它又催生了那位创作了《普特洛克勒斯⑤》的伟大艺术家：我们距离他太近了，无法正确估量他天才的神奇。现在，这艺术的酵母，又正在尼洛身上发生作用。

尼洛对于将来有着自己的梦想，不是耕种一小块土地、居住在茅草屋顶之下、被日子不如自己或者比自己

---

① 雅各布·约尔丹斯（1593—1678）：17世纪佛兰德斯最有影响力的画家之一，鲁本斯去世后，人们认为约尔丹斯是安特卫普最伟大的画家。
② 凡·艾克兄弟：扬·凡·艾克（约1385—1441）和胡伯特·凡·艾克（1370—1426），佛兰德斯画家。
③ 默兹河：西欧的一条河流，源出法国东北部，流经比利时，在荷兰西南部注入北海。
④ 第戎：法国东部城市。
⑤ 普特洛克勒斯：希腊战士，在特洛伊战争中被赫克托所杀，后友人阿基利斯为其复仇。

稍强的邻居们称作先生。安特卫普大教堂的尖顶在火红的晚霞或灰蒙蒙的黎明中耸立在原野尽头，向他传递着不同的梦想。但是这一切他都只讲给帕德拉奇听。当他们一起穿过破晓时的迷雾干活，或者休息时一起躺在水边沙沙作响的灯芯草丛中的时候，尼洛就会对着大狗的耳朵喃喃地倾诉自己天真的梦想。

因为这样的梦想很难用语言表达出来，以唤醒人类听众缓慢的同情；而且它们只会使在角落里卧床不起的可怜的老人感到极度困惑不安。就老人而言，以前每次在安特卫普的街道上行走，到小酒店里喝上一个子儿的黑啤酒，看到墙上用蓝色和红色涂抹出来的、人们称之为圣母像的画，他觉得和任何一幅著名的、画在教堂圣坛背壁的画差不多是一样的。而异乡人却要不远万里、从太阳普照之下的每一个地方来到佛兰德斯，为的是瞻仰教堂里的那些画。

除了帕德拉奇，尼洛能够倾诉自己大胆的梦想的只有一个人，这个人就是小阿洛伊斯，她住在长满青草的小坡上那座古老的红磨坊里，她的父亲是磨坊主，是村子里最有钱的农民。小阿洛伊斯只是个漂亮的小姑娘，有着温柔红润的圆脸，一双甜美的黑眼睛使她分外可爱。这种黑眼睛是西班牙人的统治留在许多佛拉芒人脸上的特征，是阿尔瓦①统治的明证，正如他们所留下的西班牙艺术在这片土地上传播的明证：宏伟的宫殿和壮观的庭院，金碧辉煌、雕梁画栋的房屋，这是纹章的历史、石头的诗篇。

小阿洛伊斯经常和尼洛及帕德拉奇在一起。他们在田野里玩耍，在雪地上奔跑，采摘雏菊和越橘。他们一同去到那座灰色的老教堂，也常常一起坐在磨坊熊熊的炉火旁。确实，小阿洛伊斯是小村里最有钱的孩子。她既没有兄弟，也没有姐妹。她穿的蓝哔叽衣服上从来没有过一个洞，过守护神节的时候，手里捧满了昂贵的坚果和糖果。当她第一次领受圣餐的时候，浅黄色的鬈发上戴着一顶镶有精致华丽的梅赫伦花边的帽子，这帽子是她外婆传给她妈妈，妈妈又传给她的。虽然她只有十二岁，人们已经在说，要是他们的儿子能够追

---

① 阿尔瓦（1507—1582）：西班牙将军，1567年血腥镇压尼德兰人民起义。历史上尼德兰包括了约为当今荷兰、比利时、卢森堡及法国东北部地区。

求并且得到她,她会是一个多么好的妻子。但她本人只是一个快乐单纯的小姑娘,丝毫也没有意识到自己可能承继的财富。她最喜爱的玩伴就是杰汉·达斯的外孙和他的狗。

第七章

有一天,阿洛伊斯的父亲科盖兹先生,一个不算坏但是有点苛刻的人,在磨坊后面长长的牧草地里偶然发现了这个可爱的小群体。那天,牧草地里的再生草刚刚被割掉。他的小女儿坐在割下的草堆里,帕德拉奇的黄色大脑袋趴在她的膝头,用虞美人和蓝色的矢车菊编成的花环环绕在他们身边。男孩尼洛用一根炭棒,正在一块干净平滑的松木板上为女孩和狗画像。

磨坊主站在那里,眼中噙着泪水,看着这幅画像。真不可思议,太像他的女儿了,而他是非常疼爱自己这个唯一的孩子的。接着,他粗暴地责备起小姑娘来,说母亲需要她在家里帮忙,而她却在这儿偷懒,要把她打发回家。女孩哭着害怕地跑了。然后,科盖兹转身从尼洛手里一把抓过松木板,"你常干这样的傻事吗?"他质问道,但是声音却有些发颤。

尼洛脸红了,他低下了头。"我看见什么就画什么。"他低声说道。

磨坊主没有说话,片刻后他伸出了手,手里捏着一个法郎。"就像我说的,画画是干傻事,白白地浪费时间,不过你画得很像阿洛伊斯,家里她母亲看到会高兴的。拿上这枚银币,把画留给我吧。"

这位阿登高地少年的脸上一下子没有了一点血色,他抬起头,把双手放在了身后。"把你的钱和这张画像都留下吧,科盖兹先生,"他直率地说,"你向来对我不错。"说完后,他把帕德拉奇叫到身边,穿过田野走了。

"我本来可以用那个法郎去看那两幅画的,"他低声对帕德拉奇说道,"可是我不能出卖她的画像,哪怕是为了那两幅画也不能。"

科盖兹先生回到他在磨坊屋的家里,心里感到十分烦恼。"不能再让那个男孩老是和阿洛伊斯在一起了,"

那天夜里，他对妻子说，"以后会有麻烦的，他已经十五岁了，她也十二岁了；男孩脸蛋很俊，身材又好。"

"而且他是个好孩子，一个忠实的信徒。"他的妻子说道，眼光热切地看着松木板上的画像。画像端踞在壁炉上方，同橡木布谷鸟自鸣钟及耶稣受难的蜡像放在一起。

"不错，我不否认这一点。"磨坊主说着，喝干了白镴酒壶里的酒。

"不过，要是你心里想的情况真会出现的话，"妻子犹犹豫豫地说道，"真有那么要紧吗？她的钱足够他们俩花的，而幸福是最重要的。"

"你是个妇道人家，所以是个傻瓜。"磨坊主用烟斗敲着桌子，狠狠地说，"那男孩就是个叫花子，再加上这种画画的人的幻想，比叫花子还不如。注意以后不要让他们在一起，否则我就会把女儿送到圣心会[①]教堂去，让修女们更好地照看她。"

可怜的母亲吓坏了，低声下气地答应按他的意愿去

---

① 圣心会：天主教女修会，1800年由修女芭拉创立于法国，后发展到全欧以及南北美洲等地。

做。倒不是说她能够硬下心肠,把女儿和她最喜欢的玩伴完全分开,甚至磨坊主也并不想对一个除了穷之外没有别的过错的少年太过残酷。但是有许多办法可以把小阿洛伊斯和她所选择的同伴分开。而尼洛作为一个自尊、文静又敏感的男孩,感情很快就受到了伤害,不再和帕德拉奇向小坡上古老的红磨坊走去,过去他一有空闲总是到那里去的。

尼洛不知道自己怎么冒犯了科盖兹先生。他猜想,在牧草地里给阿洛伊斯画像这件事不知怎的惹恼了科盖兹先生,所以当喜爱他的小姑娘跑到他身边,把手紧贴在他手心里的时候,他总是很伤感地对她一笑,怀着对她亲切的关怀说:"别这样,阿洛伊斯,别惹你父亲生气。他觉得我使你变得懒散了,亲爱的,他不喜欢你和我在一起。他是个好人,非常疼爱你,我们不要惹他生气了,阿洛伊斯。"

但是他在说这话的时候心里是很悲哀的。对他来说,世界也不像过去他在旭日东升时和帕德拉奇一起,沿着笔直的大路走在白杨树下那么明亮美好了。古老的红磨坊曾经是他的地标,来回的路上他都会在那里停留片刻，和里面的人开心地打招呼，而在低矮的磨坊小门上方，会探出她淡黄色头发的小脑袋，伸出来的红红的小手里有给帕德拉奇的一根骨头或者一块面包皮。

现在，帕德拉奇满怀渴望地看着这扇关闭着的门，而少年也不再停留，心中怀着极度的悲痛继续前行。小女孩则在屋子里，坐在炉边的小凳子上，慢慢流出的眼泪滴落在手里编织着的东西上。在磨坊机子和麻袋间忙活的科盖兹先生，则会更加坚定决心，对自己说："这样最好。那男孩差不多就是个叫花子，满脑袋没用的愚蠢空想。谁知道将来会惹出什么祸来？"

在他那一代人中间，科盖兹是个聪明人，所以，除了难得的或正式的场合之外，他绝不会敞开大门。而对这两个孩子来说，这样的场合既不令人激动也不让人高兴，因为他们久已习惯了每天快乐的、无忧无虑的、幸福的问候、交谈和玩乐。唯一看到他们的游戏、听到他们幻想的只有帕德拉奇，他带着一副聪明相摇晃着脖子上的铜铃，以一条狗所具有的同情，对他们的每一点情绪变化，做出迅速的回应。

在此期间，那块小小的松木板仍然和布谷鸟自鸣钟及耶稣受难的蜡像一起，放在磨坊屋厨房里壁炉的上方。他们接受了他的礼物，却拒绝接受他本人，有时候这似乎使尼洛感到有点难以忍受。

第八章

但是他并没有抱怨,因为他习惯于沉默。老杰汉·达斯总是对他说:"我们穷,我们必须接受上帝的赐予——好的坏的同样接受。穷人是不能选择的。"

出于对老外公的尊重,尼洛一向只是默默地听着,但是使天才儿童陶醉的某种模糊、美好的希望却在他心中低语:"可是穷人有时候是做出了选择的——选择成为一个伟大的人,这样人们就不能对他说不了。"天真单纯的尼洛仍然是这么想的。有一天,小阿洛伊斯偶然发现他独自在河边的玉米地里,便向他跑去,紧紧抱着他,可怜地哭了起来,因为第二天是她的圣徒纪念日①,她的父母没有请尼洛来参加晚宴和在大谷仓里玩耍。每年都是这样庆祝她的圣徒纪念日的,可是今年他们没有请他。尼洛吻了吻她,怀着坚定的信念低声说道:"阿洛伊斯,总有一天情况会完全不一样的。总有一天,在你父亲手里的我的那一块小松木板会有很大价值的,那时候他就不会对我关闭大门了。你只要永远爱我,亲爱的小阿洛伊斯,只要你永远爱我,我就会成为一个伟大的人。"

"要是我不爱你呢?"女性撒娇的本能使漂亮的小姑娘透过泪水、微噘着小嘴问道。

尼洛的眼睛从她脸上移开,向远方看去,安特卫普大教堂的尖顶耸立在佛拉芒金红的暮色中。他脸上的笑容是如此甜美却又如此悲伤,使小阿洛伊斯感到畏怯。"我仍然会成为一个伟大的人,"他低声说,"仍然会成为一个伟大的人,要不然就死去,阿洛伊斯。"

"那么你并不爱我!"那被宠坏了的小姑娘说着推开了尼洛。但是他微笑着摇摇头,穿过长满高高的、金黄

---

① 按天主教的习俗,孩子出生后要用某个圣徒的名字命名,该圣徒的纪念日即为这个孩子的圣徒纪念日,亦称命名日。

的玉米棵子的田地走了。在想象中他看到了美好的未来，有一天他会走进那熟悉的地方，向阿洛伊斯的家人求婚。他不但不会遭到拒绝，反而会受到隆重接待，村民们会蜂拥而至来看他，交头接耳地说："你看见了吗？他是一位人中之王，因为他是个伟大的艺术家，全世界都称颂他的大名。然而他当年只不过是我们可怜的小尼洛，可以说就是个叫花子，靠他的狗的帮助才挣到一口面包。"他想象自己会如何让外公穿着华丽的衣服和皮袍，给他画一幅画像，就像圣雅克大教堂中私人祈祷处那幅家庭画像中的老人一样。他想象要给帕德拉奇套上金项圈，让他待在自己的右手边，对大家说："有一度他曾经是我唯一的朋友。"他想象将在能够看见高耸的安特卫普大教堂尖顶的斜坡上，为自己建造一座巨大的白色大理石宫殿，以及花木茂盛的花园。他不仅自己住在里面，而且要把所有年轻、贫穷、没有朋友，但决心要做大事的人召集到这里来，就像回到家里一样。他想象，如果他们要赞美自己，他总是会这样对他们说："不，不要感谢我——感谢鲁本斯吧。没有他，就没有我的今天。"这些无法实现的梦想美丽而天真，没有任何利己的私心，充满了对英雄的崇拜，紧紧萦绕在他的心头，使他走开去的时候感到很幸福——即使在他不能参加阿洛伊斯的这个让他忧伤的圣徒纪念日的时候，他依然感到幸福。他和帕德拉奇独自回到那个黑暗的小屋的家，只有黑面包吃；而村子里所有的孩子都在磨坊屋里欢笑歌唱，吃着第戎的大圆蛋糕和布拉邦特的杏仁姜饼，在大谷仓里、在星光下、在长笛和提琴的乐声中跳舞。

"没关系，帕德拉奇，"他搂着狗的脖子坐在小屋门口，夜空里传来了磨坊屋里的欢笑声，"没关系，不久一切都会改变的。"

他寄希望于未来，而阅历更深更通世故的帕德拉奇则认为，梦想着在渺茫的未来会有牛奶和蜂蜜，根本弥补不了眼下不能去磨坊屋享受晚餐的损失。此后，每当他走过科盖兹先生的身边，帕德拉奇就会恨恨地嗥叫几声。

"今天是阿洛伊斯的命名日，对吗？"那晚，杰汉·达斯老人躺在角落里自己铺着麻袋布的床上问道。

尼洛做了个手势，表示肯定。他真希望老人的记忆出了点毛病，而不是记得这么准确。

"你怎么不去?"外公追问道,"你以前可是年年都去的,尼洛。"

"你病得太重了,不能离开人。"少年低声说道,年轻俊美的头低垂在床上。

"啧啧!福莱特大妈会来陪我的,她来过多少次了。怎么回事,尼洛?"老人继续追问道,"你该不是和小姑娘吵架了吧?"

"没有,外公,从来没有吵过架。"少年迅速回答道,低垂着的脸红了起来,"事实很简单,科盖兹先生今年没有请我去。他忽然有点讨厌起我来。"

"可是你没有做错事吧?"

"这我知道,没有。我在一块松木板上给阿洛伊斯画了一幅像,没别的。"

"哦!"老人沉默了,少年天真的回答使他明白了真相。虽然他躺在枝条做顶的小屋一角,已经离不开那张干树叶铺的床了,但是他并没有完全忘记外面的世道。

他疼爱地把尼洛满头金发的脑袋温柔地搂在怀里。"孩子,你太穷了,"他说道,苍老颤抖的声音抖得更厉害了,"这么穷!对你来说太难了。"

"不是的,我很富有。"尼洛喃喃道,天真单纯的他确实这样认为——他拥有比君王的力量更为强大的不朽的力量。他起身走到小屋的门口,静静地站立在静谧的秋夜里,望着天空密密的繁星,以及在风中摇摆的高高的白杨树。磨坊屋的每一扇窗子里都闪烁着灯光,不时能听到长笛的乐声。眼泪顺着他的面颊流了下来,毕竟他还是个孩子,然而他却笑着对自己说:"看将来吧!"

他一直待在门口,直到一切都沉寂下来,归于黑暗。这时,他才和帕德拉奇一起进到小屋里面,紧挨着睡了长长的、深沉的一觉。

第九章

现在,尼洛有了个秘密,这个秘密只有帕德拉奇知道。

他们的小屋外面有一个小棚子,除了尼洛,没有人进到里面去。这是个索然寡味的地方,但是从北面射进来的光线充足而明亮。他在这里给自己用粗木料做了个简陋的画架,上面摊着一张巨大的灰色的纸,他把占据他脑海的无数想象中的一个在纸上画了下来。从来没有人教过他画画,他也没有钱买颜料,很多次他都不得不饿着肚子,用买面包的钱买来现有这几件简陋的用具。他只能用黑白两色描绘他看到的事物。他用粉笔在这里画下的这个巨大轮廓，只不过是一个坐在一棵砍倒的树上的老人——仅此而已。他曾许多次看见，樵夫老迈克尔黄昏时就是这样坐着的。从来没有人告诉过他怎样画素描，什么是透视、解剖学，或者画面阴暗部分如何处理。然而，他把老人疲倦消瘦的老态、他的伤感和沉默的忍耐、他的粗犷、饱经忧患的悲凉一览无余地表现了出来。老人孤独的身影就是一首诗，他独自坐在枯树上沉思，身后是越来越浓的夜色。

当然，画还有些粗糙，肯定存在许多毛病。然而它真实，对自然、对艺术都是真实的，画面令人伤感，在某种程度上很美。

每天干完活以后，帕德拉奇总是安静地躺在一边，在无数个小时中看着画一点一点地创作出来。他知道尼洛心存一个希望，也许是徒劳不切实际的，但却是尼洛无比珍视的希望，那就是把这幅巨画送去参赛。安特卫普市宣布，每年举行一次绘画比赛，十八岁以下有才能的少年，不论是读书人还是庄稼汉，都可以参加，参赛者的作品必须是独立完成的粉笔画或铅笔画，奖金为二百法郎。鲁本斯之城——安特卫普——的三个顶级画家将担任裁判，根据画作的优劣选出一名获奖者。

整个春、夏、秋三季，尼洛都在画这幅珍贵的作品，如果能够得奖，他就能迈出通向独立和神秘的艺术的第一步，对于这神秘的艺术，他充满了盲目的、无知的，然而是炽烈的崇拜。

他没有把自己的心愿告诉任何人：外公不会理解他，他又失去了小阿洛伊斯，他只能对帕德拉奇述说一切。他低声说道："假如鲁本斯知道这件事，我想他会让我得奖的。"

帕德拉奇也这样想，因为他知道鲁本斯爱狗，否则他不会把狗画得这样精美逼真。而帕德拉奇知道，爱狗的人总是富有同情心的。

参赛画作要在十二月一日交上去，二十四日宣布结果，这样，获奖者就可以在圣诞节期间和家人一同庆祝。

一个寒冷的冬天，在微明的曙光中，尼洛把那巨大的画幅放在他那辆小小的绿色送奶车上，在帕德拉奇的帮助下，把画拉到了城里。他的心时而因为满怀希望而狂跳；时而又因为恐惧而变得虚弱无力。他按规定把画留在了一座公共大楼门内。

"也许我的画毫无价值。我又怎么知道呢?"他想道。他完全没有自信,感到十分沮丧。现在既然已经把画留在了那里,尼洛觉得像自己这样一个光着脚的少年,连字也认不得几个,居然梦想着能够画出让伟大的画家、真正的艺术家赏脸去看的东西来,似乎是太冒险、太自不量力、太愚蠢了。然而当他经过大教堂的时候,又重拾起了信心。鲁本斯高贵的身影仿佛从夜色和雾气中升起,赫然耸现在他面前,唇边挂着亲切的微笑,似乎在低声对他说道:"不要这样,鼓起勇气来!我不是靠懦弱和莫名的恐惧把自己的名字写在安特卫普的史册上的。"

尼洛得到了慰藉,在寒夜中跑回家去。他已经尽了最大的努力,剩下的就看上帝的旨意了,他这样想,心里满怀着天真的、从不质疑的信念,那是他在柳树和白杨掩映下的灰色小教堂里得到的教诲。

第十章

这时,冬天已经很冷了。那晚他们回到小屋后开始下雪,一连下了许多天,掩盖了小路和田垄,冰封了较小的溪流,严寒在平原上肆虐。确实,摸黑取牛奶,然后摸黑运到死寂的城市里,这工作变得异常艰苦。对帕德拉奇来说更是如此。岁月的流逝使尼洛长成一个更为壮实的少年,却使帕德拉奇进入了老年,他的关节僵硬,骨头经常酸痛。但是他绝不会放下他那份工作。尼洛不想让他干活,他要自己来拉车,但是帕德拉奇不答应。他只允许尼洛在小车笨重迟缓地在冰沟中行进的时候,在后面帮着推上一把。帕德拉奇一生都在戴着挽具拉车中度过，他为此感到自豪。严寒、难走的道路、四肢的风湿痛有时候使他非常痛苦，但他只是喘着粗气、弯着结实的脖子、坚定地忍耐着前行。

"你在家休息吧，帕德拉奇，到了你该休息的时候了，我能行，自己就能把车推进城去。"许多个早晨尼洛都这样使劲劝帕德拉奇。帕德拉奇明白他的意思，但是他不同意留在家里，就像一个老兵听见冲锋号响起时不会退缩，帕德拉奇每天都会爬起来，置身于车辕之间，缓慢而沉重地穿过积雪的田野。多少年以来，他那四个圆圆的脚掌曾在上面留下了自己的印记。

"只要活着，就绝对不能休息。"帕德拉奇想道，而有时候他似乎感觉到，这样的休息时刻离他已经不远了。他的视力不如从前了，睡一夜早晨起身的时候，身体感到疼痛。然而只要小教堂的钟声在五点钟敲响，告诉他干活的一天已经开始，他就绝不会在干草铺上多躺片刻工夫。

"我可怜的帕德拉奇，你和我很快就要躺在一起长眠了。"老杰汉·达斯说道，一面探身用苍老干枯的手抚摸帕德拉奇的头。这是一直和他分享仅有的一块干面包皮的手。同一个念头折磨着老人和老狗的心：他们离去以后，谁会来照看他们的宝贝儿呢？

一天下午，他们从安特卫普踏雪回家，整个佛拉芒平原上，积雪的地面变得和大理石一样又硬又滑。他们发现，有一个漂亮的小木偶掉在路上——一个铃鼓①手，大约六英寸高，全身大红和金黄。不像人们不小心掉落的大玩偶，这个小东西一点也没有摔坏。这是个漂亮的玩具。尼洛试图寻找他的主人，但没有找到。于是尼洛想道，这正是一件能讨得阿洛伊斯欢心的东西。

他经过磨坊屋的时候已经是夜晚了。他认识阿洛伊斯房间那扇小窗子。他想，如果他把发现的这个小物件送给她，是不会有什么不妥当的，他们毕竟在一起玩了这么长时间。在她窗子下面有一个小棚子，棚顶是斜的，他爬上棚顶，轻轻地敲敲窗格子。屋子里有微弱的灯光。小姑娘打开窗户有点害怕地向外面张望。

尼洛把铃鼓手放在她手里，低声说道："给你，这是我在雪地里拾到的一个玩偶，阿洛伊斯。拿着吧，愿上

---

① 铃鼓：蒙有塑料或皮面，鼓帮装有金属圆片，摇动或用手击打发声。

帝保佑你，亲爱的！"

没等她来得及谢谢他，尼洛就从棚子顶上出溜了下去，在黑暗中跑掉了。

那天晚上，磨坊发生了火灾，虽然磨坊本身和住房没有遭殃，但是院子里其他建筑和不少玉米被烧毁了。全村人都惊恐万分地跑出来，救火车冒雪飞速从安特卫普赶来。磨坊主是保了险的，不会有什么损失，但他还是暴跳如雷，声称这场大火并非意外，而是有人出于某种罪恶目的放的。

尼洛从睡梦中惊醒，和其他人一起跑去救火，但是科盖兹先生怒冲冲地把他推到了一边。"你天黑以后在这里逛来逛去的，"他粗暴地说道，"我敢发誓，你比别人都更清楚火灾是怎么回事。"

尼洛听见这话惊呆了，他一声不吭，没有料到有人会说出这样的话来，除非是开玩笑，而他也不明白，谁能够在这样的时候开玩笑。

但是，磨坊主在第二天公开地对许多邻居说出了这蛮不讲理的话。虽然没有对这个少年提出认真的指控，但流言却散布了开来，说那天天黑以后，尼洛被人看见在磨坊院里不知干些什么勾当，说科盖兹先生禁止他和小阿洛伊斯交往，因而他对科盖兹先生怀恨在心。而村里人一向都是俯首帖耳地听从最有钱的财主的话，都希望在将来的某一天，他们的儿子能够获得阿洛伊斯的财富，于是都心领神会，对老杰汉·达斯的外孙冷眼相看，冷语相加。

没有人公开地对尼洛说些什么，但是村民都一致顺从了磨坊主的偏见，尼洛和帕德拉奇每天早晨都要到一些农舍和农场去收牛奶往安特卫普送，原先那里的人们对他们都是笑脸相迎，快乐地打招呼，而现在这些人都低着头，眼睛朝下，说话也只是只言片语。没有人真正相信磨坊主荒唐的怀疑，也没有人相信由此而生的对尼洛的蛮横指责，但是他们都极其贫穷，十分无知，而当地唯一的有钱人已经明确表示了对尼洛的反感，因此，无辜又无助的尼洛根本没有力量阻挡这股逆流。

"你对那个孩子太残酷了，"磨坊主的妻子壮起胆子，一面哭着一面对丈夫说，"他绝对是个天真可靠的孩子，无论内心多么痛苦，也绝不会想出这种坏主意的。"

但是科盖兹先生是个固执的人，话一旦说出来就死不改口，虽然在内心深处他也知道自己这样做很不公平。

在此期间，尼洛忍受着对他的伤害，他具有的自尊宽容使他不屑于去叫屈，只有和老帕德拉奇单独相处的时候才会稍有不同。他不去叫屈还有另外一个原因，那就是他想："如果我的画得了奖，也许那时候他们就会感到懊悔了。"

然而，对于一个不到十六岁的男孩子来说，他短短的人生是在同一个小小世界度过，这个世界从各个方面给了他爱抚和夸赞，而如今却无缘无故地站在了他的对立面，这是多么痛苦的考验啊！特别是在那个凄凉萧瑟、冰天雪地、饥寒交迫的冬天，就更加痛苦了。因为这种时候，只有在村舍的炉边和邻居友爱的问候中，才能获得唯一的光明和温暖。

冬季使人们的关系更为密切，大家相互之间都这样，除了对尼洛和帕德拉奇。现在谁也不愿意和他们有什么来往，听任他们和小屋里那个瘫痪了的、卧床不起的老人挣扎着过日子。小屋里炉火经常十分微弱，桌上经常没有面包，因为从安特卫普来了一个收购牛奶的人，开始每天赶着骡子到各家去收牛奶，只剩下三四户人家拒绝接受他的收购价，继续让尼洛的小绿车送奶去卖。这样一来，帕德拉奇拉的分量变得很轻，而尼洛钱袋里的生丁①，唉！也同样变得很少了。

帕德拉奇会一如既往地在所有熟悉的门口停下来，但是现在门不再为他打开。他会满怀渴望地看着这些门，发出无声的呼吁。关闭了他们的大门和心扉、听任帕德拉奇拉着空车离去的邻居们心里感到痛楚，但他们还是这样做了，因为他们希望讨好科盖兹先生。

---

① 生丁：一百生丁为一法郎。

第十一章

马上就要过圣诞节了。

天气糟透了,冷得要命。雪足足有六英尺深,冰冻得十分结实,人和牛可以在上面随意行走。在这样的节日期间里,小村总是喜气洋洋的。即使在最穷困的房子里,都会有牛奶甜酒以及糕饼,人们开玩笑、跳舞,有裹着糖衣的圣徒像和涂成金色的耶稣像。到处都能听到马脖子上佛兰德斯铃铛的叮咚声;每一扇门里都有盛得满满的汤锅在火炉上冒着热气欢唱;外面雪地里到处都有欢笑的少女,她们戴着鲜艳的头巾,穿着厚厚的袍子,急匆匆地去教堂做弥撒或者做完弥撒出来。只有那间小屋里是又黑又冷。

现在,尼洛和帕德拉奇真的是完完全全被孤苦伶仃地留在世界上了,因为圣诞节前一周的一个夜晚,死神进入了小屋,永远带走了老杰汉·达斯。老人一生经受的只有贫穷和痛苦。很久以来他已经是半死不活的了,除了做个无力的手势,哪儿也不能动,只有轻声吐出一个字的力气。然而他的去世,仍然使他们俩感到十分恐惧,使他们非常悲伤。他是在睡梦中离开他们的,当他们在灰蒙蒙的清晨知道失去了亲人,难以言表的孤独和凄凉仿佛从四面八方把他们包围了起来。长久以来,他只不过是个贫穷、衰弱、瘫痪的老人,根本不能保护他们,但是他深深爱着他们。他总是用微笑欢迎他们的归来。

在那个苍白的冬日,当他们跟在放着老人遗体的松木棺材后面,向灰色小教堂旁边的无名墓地走去的时候,他们一直哀伤不已,谁也无法安慰他们。唯一来给老人送葬的,是被他无依无靠地留在这个世界上的少年和老狗。"现在他想必会发善心,允许那可怜的孩子到我们这儿来了吧?"磨坊主的妻子看了一眼坐在壁炉旁吸烟的丈夫,心里想道。

科盖兹先生知道她在想些什么,但是他硬起心肠,当这小小的、卑微的出殡行列经过他家的时候,他没有打开他家的大门。"那男孩就是个要饭的,"他对自己说,"决不许他和阿洛伊斯来往。"

女人不敢说什么,但是当坟上的土埋好,两个送葬者离开以后,她给了阿洛伊斯一个蜡菊花圈,叫她把花圈恭恭敬敬地放在那个铲掉了积雪的、没有墓碑的黑色土堆上。

尼洛和帕德拉奇怀着破碎的心回到了家里。但是即使在这个贫穷、忧郁、没有欢乐的家里,他们也得不到任何安慰。这个小房子他们已经欠了一个月的房租,而当尼洛为死者举行了可怜的葬礼后,已经一分钱都没有了。他去求房东宽限一下,房东是个修鞋匠,每星期日晚上都要和科盖兹先生一起喝酒抽烟。这是个爱钱如命的苛刻的守财奴,当然不肯通融。他声称,小屋里的每一样东西,所有的盆盆罐罐,都要用来顶替拖欠的房租,让尼洛和帕德拉奇第二天就离开。

说起来,小屋是够简陋,而且在某种意义上说够悲惨的了，然而他们的心却对它有着无限的依恋。他们曾幸福地生活在那里。夏天，小屋上爬满常春藤和开花的豆类植物，四周是阳光灿烂的田野，真是又鲜亮又好看。小屋里面的生活是辛劳困苦的，然而当他们一起跑向那老人，迎接他那永远浮现在脸上的欢迎的微笑的时候，他们曾感到这样的满足，心里是这样的快乐。

整整一夜，少年和狗在黑暗中坐在没有火的炉子旁，他们悲伤地紧紧依偎在一起取暖。他们的身体对寒冷已经麻木了，他们的心似乎冻结了。

当黎明降临这片寒冷的冰雪覆盖的大地时，正是圣诞节前夜的清晨。尼洛一阵战栗，紧紧地抱住了他唯一的朋友，热泪涌出，滴落在帕德拉奇坦诚的前额上。"咱们走吧，帕德拉奇——亲爱的、亲爱的帕德拉奇，"他喃喃道，"别等着人家把我们踢出大门，咱们走吧。"

帕德拉奇完全听从他的意愿，他们伤心地并排走出了他们深爱的小屋，对他们来说，里面的每一件琐碎简朴的东西都是宝贵的，他们珍爱这里的一切。帕德拉奇走过自己那辆绿色小车的时候消沉地垂下了头：小车不再是他的了——必须和其他的东西一起抵债，他的铜挽具闲躺在雪地上，闪闪发光。帕德拉奇本可以躺在挽具旁，伤心而死，但是只要少年活着并且需要他，帕德拉奇就不会屈服，不会放弃。

他们循着走惯了的老路走向安特卫普。天也就刚刚破晓，大多数的百叶窗还关着，但是有些村民已经开始活动了。男孩和大狗走过他们身边的时候，这些人没有理会他们。尼洛经过一个门口的时候，充满渴望地向门里看去：他的外公曾经给住在里面的邻居帮过许多忙。

"你能给帕德拉奇一块面包皮吗？"他怯生生地说，"他老了，从昨天上午到现在什么东西都没有吃过。"

女人急忙关上了门，含混地嘟哝说，这个季节小麦和黑麦都很贵。男孩和狗疲倦无力地继续往前走去，他们不再问人要吃的了。

钟声敲响十点的时候，他们缓慢而吃力地来到了安特卫普。

"要是我身上有什么东西可以卖了给他买个面包就好了！"尼洛心里想道。但是除了用以蔽体的那点亚麻和哔叽衣裤以及一双木鞋之外，他是一无所有了。

帕德拉奇很理解男孩，他把鼻子放在他的手心里，似乎在恳求男孩不要为他的任何苦恼和需求而烦恼不安。

那天中午要宣布绘画比赛得奖者的名字,尼洛朝他送交了自己珍贵的画作的那座公共大楼走去。大楼的台阶上和门廊里有一群年轻人,有的和他一样大,有的年纪大一些,都有父母或亲朋好友和他们在一起。尼洛紧挨着帕德拉奇来到他们中间的时候,心里害怕得要命。城里的大钟响亮刺耳地撞响了正午的时刻。通向内厅的门打开了,充满渴望的、气喘吁吁的人群蜂拥而入。大家都知道,获奖的作品将会放置在一个木头台子上,高出参赛的其余画作。

尼洛的视线蒙眬起来,他头昏眼花,四肢无力。当他的视力重新逐渐清晰起来以后,他看见那幅高高在上的画不是他自己的!一个洪亮的声音正在缓慢地大声宣布,获奖者是斯蒂芬·斯吉林格,出生于安特卫普市,是该市一个码头老板的儿子。

第十二章

尼洛苏醒过来的时候,发现自己躺在门外的石子路上,帕德拉奇正试图运用他拥有的一切办法来唤醒他。远处,安特卫普的一群年轻人围在他们得胜的同伴身边高声喊叫,欢呼着,簇拥着他回到码头上的家里去。

少年摇摇晃晃地站立起来,把狗拉进怀里搂着。"完了,亲爱的帕德拉奇,"他喃喃道,"全完了!"

他尽可能使自己振作起来,按原路往村子走去。他已经饿得没有什么力气了,帕德拉奇耷拉着脑袋在他身边慢慢走着,衰老的四肢因饥饿和悲伤而虚弱无力。

雪下得很紧,飓风从北面猛烈刮来,平原上冷得要死。他们花了很长的时间才走完这段熟悉的路程,当他们走近小村的时候,钟声正敲响四点。突然,帕德拉奇在雪中闻到了一种气味,他停住脚,用爪子扒拉着雪,嘴里发出呜呜的声音,然后用牙齿叼出了一个棕色的小皮钱包。他在黑暗中把钱包高高叼起朝向尼洛。在他们站立的地方有一个小小的耶稣受难的十字架,十字架下面点着一盏昏暗的灯,男孩机械地把钱包放到灯光下,钱包上有科盖兹先生的名字,里面有两千法郎的钞票。

眼前的景象使尼洛稍稍摆脱了恍惚的状态,他把钱包塞进衬衫,抚摸了一下帕德拉奇,领着他继续往前走。帕德拉奇满怀渴望地抬头看着他的脸。

尼洛笔直地朝磨坊屋走去,他走到门口,使劲敲门。磨坊主的妻子眼泪汪汪地开了门,小阿洛伊斯紧跟在她身后。"是你吗,可怜的孩子?"她透过泪眼和蔼地说道,"别等科盖兹先生看见你,赶快离开这儿吧。我们今天晚上有大麻烦了。他今天在骑马回家的路上遗失了一大笔钱,现在出去找了,在这样的大雪天他永远也不会找到的。上帝知道,这几乎会毁了我们的。这是老天因为我们对你所做的事而惩罚我们。"

尼洛把钱包放在她的手里，把帕德拉奇叫到房子里面来，"今晚是帕德拉奇发现的钱包，"他急速说道，"告诉科盖兹先生这一点，我想他不会拒绝给已经年老的帕德拉奇食物和一个遮风避雨的地方。看住他别让他跟着我，求你们好好待他。"

在女人和狗明白他的意思之前，他已经俯身亲吻了帕德拉奇，然后急忙关上了门，消失在迅速降临的夜色中。

女人和姑娘站在那里，喜悦和恐惧使她们一句话也说不出来。帕德拉奇则徒劳地将满腔痛苦发泄在上了门闩的包铁的橡木门上。她们不敢打开门闩放他出去。她们想尽一切办法安慰他。她们给他拿来了甜糕饼和多汁的肉类，用她们拥有的最好的东西来吸引他，她们试图逗引他待在温暖的壁炉旁，但是一切都是枉费心机。帕德拉奇拒绝她们的安慰，一步也不离开闩着的大门。

当磨坊主终于走进后门，来到妻子身边的时候，已经是六点钟了。他精疲力竭、无比沮丧，"永远找不回来了，"他面如死灰，严厉的声音中带着颤抖，"我们打着灯笼四处都找遍了，没找到——女儿的嫁妆等等一切都完了!"

他的妻子把钱包放在他的手里,并告诉他这钱是怎么回来的。这个强壮的男人颤抖着跌坐下来,又羞又怕地捂住了脸。"我对这孩子太残酷了,"最后,他终于嘟哝道,"我不配得到他这么好的对待。"

小阿洛伊斯鼓起勇气,轻轻走到父亲身边,把有着金色鬈发的头依偎在他身上。"尼洛可以来这儿了吧,爸爸?"她轻声说道,"明天他就可以和以前一样来这儿了吧?"

磨坊主用胳膊紧搂着她,他那冷酷的、被太阳晒得黑黑的脸这时十分苍白,他的嘴抖动着。"当然啦,当然啦,"他回答女儿道,"让他明天来过圣诞节,只要他愿意,哪天都可以来。上帝帮助我,我要补偿他——我一定要补偿他。"

小阿洛伊斯充满感激和快乐地亲吻了他,然后从他膝头上出溜下来,跑到仍守望在门旁的帕德拉奇身边。"今晚我可以给帕德拉奇大吃一顿了?"她大声说道,真是个孩子,快乐起来就不顾一切了。

她的父亲庄重地低下头说:"当然,当然,要拿最好的东西给他吃。"这个苛刻的老头深为感动,内心深处受到了极大的震撼。

这天正是圣诞前夜,磨坊屋里放满了橡木木柴和一方方泥炭,奶油和蜂蜜,肉类和面包,橡子上面挂着常青植物编成的花环,耶稣受难像和布谷鸟自鸣钟四周装饰着大量的冬青。还有专门为阿洛伊斯挂起来的小小的纸灯笼,各种各样的玩具和用鲜艳的印花糖纸包着的糖果。屋子里到处明亮、温暖、富足,女孩非常想把帕德拉奇当作尊贵的客人来款待。

但是帕德拉奇既不肯躺在温暖的地方,也不肯分享他们的快乐。他确实又饿又冷,但是没有尼洛,他不愿单独享受舒适,也不愿吃什么东西。任何诱惑都打动不了他,他总是紧靠在门边,一心寻找着逃跑的办法。

"他要的是那男孩,"科盖兹先生说,"真是好狗!好狗!明天天一亮,我第一件事就是去男孩家。"事实上,除了帕德拉奇,谁也不知道尼洛已经离开了那座小屋;除了帕德拉奇,谁也没有猜到尼洛离开是为了独自去面对饥饿和痛苦。

第十三章

　　磨坊屋里的厨房非常暖和。大块的木柴在壁炉里烧得噼啪作响，腾起熊熊火焰。邻居们都来喝上一杯酒，吃一片为晚餐烤制的肥鹅。阿洛伊斯相信自己的玩伴第二天一定会回到这里来，她兴奋极了，又跳又唱，不断向后甩动着金发。科盖兹先生透过湿漉漉的双眼，满心欢喜地对女儿微笑着，并且说起他将会怎样帮助她最喜爱的伙伴。母亲平静地坐在纺车前，一脸心满意足的神情。自鸣钟里的布谷鸟叽叽喳喳地欢乐地叫着报时。在这欢快的氛围中，人们一再欢迎帕德拉奇作为贵客留下来。但是，无论是安宁还是富足，都不能把他引诱到没有尼洛在场的地方去。

当晚餐在餐桌上冒着热气,欢声笑语最为响亮、圣子耶稣给阿洛伊斯带来了精选的最好的礼物的时候,一直在注意寻找机会的帕德拉奇,趁一个粗心的新来客没有闩上大门,一下子就悄悄溜了出去,使出他疲乏虚弱的四肢的全部力气,奔跑在寒冷的黑夜里的雪地上。他只有一个念头,那就是追赶尼洛。如果你的朋友是人类的一员,他可能会为这可口的一餐、惬意的温暖、舒适的睡眠而停下脚步,但这可不是帕德拉奇理解的友谊。他记得过去的一个时刻,那时,一个老人和一个小孩子在路边的水沟里发现了病得要死的他。

整整一晚都在下雪,这时已经快十点钟了,男孩的足迹几乎完全消失了。帕德拉奇花了很长时间才发现了一丝尼洛的气味。但当他终于找到的时候,却又很快消失了。失而复得,得而复失,反反复复,一百次都不止。

那夜天气十分恶劣。路边十字架下面的灯都被吹灭了。路面上是一层冰。无法穿透的黑暗掩盖了人类居住的任何痕迹,没有任何有生命的东西在外面活动。牲口全都进了圈,在所有的小屋和宅院里,男男女女都在尽情欢庆、大吃大喝。在这严酷的寒夜里,只有帕德拉奇待在外面。他又老又饿,浑身疼痛,但是伟大的爱给了他力量和坚忍,支撑着他不断搜寻下去。

尼洛的足迹覆盖在新雪之下,尽管十分模糊不清,但能够辨出是一直沿着他们习惯走的路径去到了安特卫普。帕德拉奇追踪着足迹,进入城市,走进狭窄、弯曲、昏暗的街道的时候,已经是午夜过后了。城里很黑,只从有些房子的百叶窗缝里闪出微红的灯光;时不时地,几个人提着灯笼、哼着喝酒的小曲走回家。路面白白的,都结了一层冰,在路面的映衬下,屋顶和高墙隐隐呈现出一片黑色。万籁俱寂,只有狂风扫过街巷时,把招牌和高高的铸铁街灯刮得摇摆震颤,嘎吱作响。

有这么多的行人在雪地上踩来踩去,这么多不同的小径相互穿来穿去,帕德拉奇想要盯紧他跟踪的足迹太困难了。但是,虽然寒冷刺骨,高低不平的冰划伤了他的脚,饥饿如老鼠的牙齿般咬噬着他,他仍然继续往前行走。这可怜的、骨瘦如柴的、浑身颤抖的东西走啊走,经过长时间耐心地追踪,终于跟随着他热爱的足迹走进了安特卫普市中心,爬上了大教堂的台阶。

"他到他热爱的东西那儿去了。"帕德拉奇想道。他弄不明白,但是他对男孩的那份对艺术的激情充满了忧伤和怜悯,这激情对于他来说无法理解,却又无比神圣。

午夜弥撒后,大教堂的门没有关上。或许是因为看守大意了,急于回家饱餐一顿或上床睡觉;也可能是他们太困了,不知道有没有拧好钥匙,就这样,有一扇门没有锁上。由于这个意外,帕德拉奇跟踪的那脚印穿过了大门,进入教堂里面,在黑色的石头地面上留下了冰雪的白色印记。这条落地就冻住了的细细的白线指引着帕德拉奇穿过无边的寂静,穿过穹隆下巨大的空间,一直来到圣坛旁的高坛的门口。他发现尼洛躺在那儿的石台上。他轻轻走上前,触摸男孩的脸。这无声的爱抚仿佛在说:"你以为我会不忠实于你、抛弃你吗?我,一条忠狗,会吗?"

男孩低叫着抬起了身子,紧紧抱住了帕德拉奇。"让我们躺下一起死去吧,"他喃喃道,"人们不需要我们,只剩下我们俩了。"

作为回答,帕德拉奇更加靠近了尼洛,把头倚在了少年的胸口,悲哀的棕色眼睛里含着大滴泪珠,他不是为自己感到悲哀,他自己是幸福的。

他们在刺骨的寒冷中紧紧挨着躺在一起。从北方海上刮来、扫过佛拉芒海堤的狂风就像一波又一波的冰浪,把触及的每一个有生命的东西统统冻结住了。他们躺在里面的那巨大的拱顶石室,比外面大雪覆盖的平原更加冷得刺骨。时不时会有一只蝙蝠在黑影中活动,时不时也会有一线亮光照到那排雕像上。尼洛和帕德拉奇一动不动地躺在鲁本斯的画作下面,寒冷令他们麻木了,就像把他们送入了梦乡。他们一起梦见过去的快乐时光,那时,他们在夏季牧场鲜花盛开的草丛中互相追逐,或者躲坐在水边高高的香蒲草中,观看船只在阳光下驶向大海。

没有任何的气恼拆散过他们,也没有任何乌云笼罩过他们的友谊。一方有情有义,另一方忠贞不贰,使他们完美的友爱和信任从未蒙上过阴影。在他们短暂的一生中,他们尽到了自己的职责,愉快地生活着。他们从不嫉妒别的人和别的动物。他们很天真，所以感到很满足。在这夜深人静的漫长的圣诞夜，当他们躺在那儿，饥饿以及血管里缓慢流动的冰冷的血液使他们虚弱昏厥的时候，出现在他们梦中的，正是这段他们共同度过的岁月。

突然，一道强烈的银光穿透黑暗，照进广阔的通道侧廊，已经升到了最高点的月亮这时冲破了云层。雪已经停了，教堂外面，积雪反射出的光清澈如黎明时的曙光。清光穿过穹形门窗照在墙上的两幅画作上，遮盖画幅的幕布已经被男孩在进门时撩开了。霎时间，《升起十字架》和《基督下十字架》清晰可见。

尼洛站立起来，伸开双臂向着那两幅画，苍白的脸上闪着狂喜的泪光。"我终于看见它们了！"他大声叫喊道，"啊，上帝，这就足够了！"

他的双腿支持不住了，他跪倒下来，仍旧抬头仰望着他崇拜的杰作。在短暂的片刻中，清光照亮了长久以来他都无法看到的神圣画面——这道清光清澈美妙又强烈，仿佛是从天国的宝座倾注下来的。然后，它突然消失了。巨大的黑暗又一次蒙住了基督的脸。

男孩的双臂再次抱紧了帕德拉奇的身体。"我们会看到基督的脸的——在那个地方,"他喃喃道,"我想,他是不会让我们分开的。"

第十四章

第二天，人们在安特卫普大教堂圣坛旁的高坛处发现了尼洛和帕德拉奇。他们都已经死了，夜间的酷寒把年轻和年老的两个生命都冻僵了。当圣诞节的早晨来临、牧师们进入教堂时，他们看见他们俩就这样一起躺在石台上。高坛上方蒙在鲁本斯巨作上的幕布已经被揭开，朝阳的霞光照在了基督戴着荆冠的头上。

过了一些时候，来了一个面貌严峻的老人，他哭得像个女人一样。"我对那个少年太残酷了，"他喃喃道，"我本来要对他做出补偿的——是的，要把我一半的财产给他——对于我来说，他本来应该像个儿子一样的。"

这一天，很快又过了些时候，一位世界著名的画家也来到了这里，他是个慷慨而开明的人。"我在寻找一个更有资格获取昨天那个绘画比赛奖的人，"他对大家说，"一个具有罕见天才和无限前途的男孩。一个老樵夫在黄昏时刻坐在一棵倒下的树上——这就是他画作的整个主题，其中却预示着伟大的未来。我想找到他，把他带走，教他画画。"

还有一个满头金色鬈发的小女孩悲伤地哭泣着，她紧抓着父亲的胳膊大声说道："啊，尼洛，回来吧！我们已经为你准备好了一切。圣子基督的手里满是礼物，老风笛手将为我们演奏，妈妈说，在圣诞节整个一周里，你将坐在壁炉旁，和我们一起烤坚果吃——是的，甚至去参加最为盛大的宴会！帕德拉奇会多么高兴啊！啊，尼洛，醒醒吧，回来吧！"

但是那张年轻苍白的脸上带着微笑、仰望着伟大的鲁本斯的光辉杰作，他对所有的人都做出了回答："一切都太晚了。"

响亮悦耳的钟声响彻严寒的大地，阳光照射在白雪覆盖的平原上，人们成群结队欢快地穿行在大街小巷间,但是尼洛和帕德拉奇再也不向他们祈求施舍了。他们现在所需要的一切,安特卫普都自发地给予了他们。

和在人世间更为长久一些的生命相比,对于他们,死亡要慈悲得多。他们一个充满了忠贞的爱心,另一个满怀着天真的信念,死神接纳了他们,将他们带离了一个爱心得不到报答、信念没办法实现的世界。

他们终生相守在一起,死后也没有分离:人们发现他们的时候,男孩的胳膊紧抱着帕德拉奇,不用大力气就无法分开。小村里的人们悔恨不已,羞愧难当,为他们祈求上帝的荣光,为他们造了一个合葬墓,让他们并排躺在里面安息——天长地久,永远相守。

A DOG OF FLANDERS

OUIDA

Contents

Chapter Ⅰ ································· 81

Chapter Ⅱ ································· 86

Chapter Ⅲ ································· 93

Chapter Ⅳ ································· 99

Chapter Ⅴ ································· 106

Chapter Ⅵ ································· 113

Chapter Ⅶ ································· 119

Chapter Ⅷ ································· 125

Chapter Ⅸ ································· 132

Chapter Ⅹ ································· 137

Chapter Ⅺ ································· 146

Chapter Ⅻ ································· 154

Chapter ⅩⅢ ································· 160

Chapter ⅩⅣ ································· 168

Chapter I

Nello and Patrasche were left all alone in the world.

They were friends in a friendship closer than brotherhood. Nello was a little Ardennois—Patrasche was a big Fleming. They were both of the same age by length of years, yet one was still young, and the other was already old. They had dwelt together almost all their days: both were orphaned and destitute, and owed their lives to the same hand. It had been the beginning of the tie between them, their first bond of sympathy; and it had strengthened day by day, and had grown with their growth, firm and indissoluble, until they loved one another very greatly.

Their home was a little hut on the edge of a little village—a Flemish village a league from Antwerp, set amidst flat breadths of pasture and corn-lands, with long lines of poplars and of alders bending in the breeze on the edge of the great canal which ran through it. It had about a score of houses and homesteads, with shutters of bright green or sky-blue, and roofs rose-red or black and white, and walls whitewashed until they shone in the sun like snow.

In the centre of the village stood a windmill, placed on a little moss-grown slope: it was a landmark to all the level country round. It had once been painted scarlet, sails and all, but that had been in its infancy, half a century or more earlier, when it had ground wheat for the soldiers of Napoleon; and it was now a ruddy brown, tanned by wind and weather. It went queerly by fits and starts, as though rheumatic and stiff in the joints from age, but it served the whole neighborhood, which would have thought it almost as impious to carry grain elsewhere as to attend any other religious service than the mass that was performed at the altar of the little old gray church, with its conical steeple, which stood opposite to it, and whose single bell rang morning, noon, and night with that strange, subdued, hollow sadness which every bell that hangs in the Low Countries seems to gain as an integral part of its melody.

Within sound of the little melancholy clock almost from their birth upward, they had dwelt together, Nello and Patrasche, in the little hut on the edge of the village, with the cathedral spire of Antwerp rising in the northeast, beyond the great green plain of seeding grass and spreading corn that stretched away from them like a tideless, changeless sea. It was the hut of a very old man, of a very poor man—of old Jehan Daas, who in his time had been a soldier, and who remembered the wars that had trampled the country as oxen tread down the furrows, and who had brought from his service nothing except a wound, which had made him a cripple.

When old Jehan Daas had reached his full eighty, his daughter had died in the Ardennes, hard by Stavelot, and had left him in legacy her two-year-old son. The old man could ill contrive to support himself, but he took up the additional burden uncomplainingly, and it soon became welcome and precious to him. Little Nello—which was but a pet diminutive for Nicolas—throve with him, and the old man and the little child lived in the poor little hut contentedly.

It was a very humble little mud-hut indeed, but it was clean and white as a seashell, and stood in a small plot of garden-ground that yielded beans and herbs and pumpkins. They were very poor, terribly poor—many a day they had nothing at all to eat. They never by any chance had enough: to have had enough to eat would have been to have reached paradise at once. But the old man was very gentle and good to the boy, and the boy was a beautiful, innocent, truthful, tender-hearted creature; and they were happy on a crust and a few leaves of cabbage, and asked no more of earth or heaven; save indeed that Patrasche should be always with them, since without Patrasche where would they have been?

For Patrasche was their alpha and omega; their treasury and granary; their store of gold and wand of wealth; their breadwinner and minister; their only friend and comforter. Patrasche dead or gone from them, they must have laid themselves down and died likewise. Patrasche was body, brains, hands, head, and feet to both of them: Patrasche was their very life, their very soul. For Jehan Daas was old and a cripple, and Nello was but a child; and Patrasche was their dog.

Chapter II

A dog of Flanders—yellow of hide, large of head and limb, with wolflike ears that stood erect, and legs bowed and feet widened in the muscular development wrought in his breed by many generations of hard service, Patrasche came of a race which had toiled hard and cruelly from sire to son in Flanders many a century—slaves of slaves, dogs of the people, beasts of the shafts and the harness, creatures that lived straining their sinews in the gall of the cart, and died breaking their hearts on the flints of the streets.

Patrasche had been born of parents who had

labored hard all their days over the sharp-set stones of the various cities and the long, shadowless, weary roads of the two Flanders and of Brabant. He had been born to no other heritage than those of pain and of toil. He had been fed on curses and baptized with blows. Why not? It was a Christian country, and Patrasche was but a dog. Before he was fully grown he had known the bitter gall of the cart and the collar. Before he had entered his thirteenth month he had become the property of a hardware-dealer, who was accustomed to wander over the land north and south, from the blue sea to the green mountains. They sold him for a small price, because he was so young.

This man was a drunkard and a brute. The life of Patrasche was a life of hell. To deal the tortures of hell on the animal creation is a way which the Christians have of showing their belief in it. His purchaser was a sullen, ill-living, brutal Brabantois, who heaped his cart full with pots and pans and flagons and buckets, and other wares of crockery and brass and tin, and left Patrasche to draw the load as best he might, whilst he himself lounged idly by the side in fat and sluggish ease, smoking his black pipe and stopping at every wineshop or cafe on the road.

Happily for Patrasche—or unhappily—he was very strong: he came of an iron race, long born and bred to such cruel travail; so that he did not die, but managed to drag on a wretched existence under the brutal burdens, the scarifying lashes, the hunger, the thirst, the blows, the curses, and the exhaustion which are the only wages with which the Flemings repay the most patient and laborious of all their four-footed victims.

One day, after two years of this long and deadly agony, Patrasche was going on as usual along one of the straight, dusty, unlovely roads that lead to the city of Rubens. It was full midsummer, and very warm. His cart was very heavy, piled high with goods in metal and in earthenware. His owner sauntered on without noticing him otherwise than by the crack of the whip as it curled round his quivering loins. The Brabantois had paused to drink beer himself at every wayside house, but he had forbidden Patrasche to stop a moment for a draught from the canal. Going along thus, in the full sun, on a scorching highway, having eaten nothing for twenty-four hours, and, which was far worse to him, not having tasted water for near twelve, being blind with dust, sore with blows, and stupefied with the merciless weight which dragged upon his loins, Patrasche staggered and foamed a little at the mouth, and fell.

He fell in the middle of the white, dusty road, in the full glare of the sun; he was sick unto death, and motionles. His master gave him the only medicine in his pharmacy—kicks and oaths and blows with a cudgel of oak, which had been often the only food and drink, the only wage and reward, ever offered to him. But Patrasche was beyond the reach of any torture or of any curses. Patrasche lay, dead to all appearances, down in the white powder of the summer dust. After a while, finding it useless to assail his ribs with punishment and his ears with maledictions, the Brabantois—deeming life gone in him, or going so nearly that his carcass was forever useless, unless indeed, some one should strip it of the skin for gloves—cursed him fiercely in farewell, struck off the leathern bands of the harness, kicked his body aside into the grass, and, groaning and muttering in savage wrath, pushed the cart lazily along the road uphill, and left the dying dog for the ants to sting and for the crows to pick.

It was the last day before Kermesse away at Louvain, and the Brabantois was in haste to reach the fair and get a good place for his truck of brass wares. He was in fierce wrath, because Patrasche had been a strong and much-enduring animal, and because he himself had now the hard task of pushing his charette all the way to Louvain. But to stay to look after Patrasche never entered his thoughts: the beast was dying and useless, and he would steal, to replace him, the first large dog that he found wandering alone out of sight of its master. Patrasche had cost him nothing, or next to nothing, and for two long, cruel years had made him toil ceaselessly in his service from sunrise to sunset, through summer and winter, in fair weather and foul.

He had got a fair use and a good profit out of Patrasche: being human, he was wise, and left the dog to draw his last breath alone in the ditch, and have his bloodshot eyes plucked out as they might be by the birds, whilst he himself went on his way to beg and to steal, to eat and to drink, to dance and to sing, in the mirth at Louvain. A dying dog, a dog of the cart—why should he waste hours over its agonies at peril of losing a handful of copper coins, at peril of a shout of laughter?

Patrasche lay there, flung in the grass-green ditch. It was a busy road that day, and hundreds of people, on foot and on mules, in wagons or in carts, went by, tramping quickly and joyously on to Louvain. Some saw him, most did not even look: all passed on. A dead dog more or less—it was nothing in Brabant: it would be nothing anywhere in the world.

Chapter III

After a time, among the holiday makers, there came a little old man who was bent and lame, and very feeble. He was in no guise for feasting: he was very poorly and miserably clad, and he dragged his silent way slowly through the dust among the pleasure-seekers. He looked at Patrasche, paused, wondered, turned aside, then kneeled down in the rank grass and weeds of the ditch, and surveyed the dog with kindly eyes of pity. There was with him a little rosy, fair-haired, dark-eyed child of a few years old, who pattered in amidst the bushes, for him breast-high, and stood gazing with a pretty seriousness upon the poor, great, quiet beast.

Thus it was that these two first met—the little Nello and the big Patrasche.

The upshot of that day was, that old Jehan Daas, with much laborious effort, drew the sufferer homeward to his own little hut, which was a stone's throw off amidst the fields, and there tended him with so much care that the sickness, which had been a brain seizure, brought on by heat and thirst and exhaustion, with time and shade and rest passed away, and health and strength returned, and Patrasche staggered up again upon his four stout, tawny legs.

Now for many weeks he had been useless, powerless, sore, near to death; but all this time he had heard no rough word, had felt no harsh touch, but only the pitying murmurs of the child's voice and the soothing caress of the old man's hand.

In his sickness they two had grown to care for him, this lonely man and the little happy child. He had a corner of the hut, with a heap of dry grass for his bed; and they had learned to listen eagerly for his breathing in the dark night, to tell them that he lived; and when he first was well enough to essay a loud, hollow, broken bay, they laughed aloud, and almost wept together for joy at such a sign of his sure restoration; and little Nello, in delighted glee, hung round his rugged neck with chains of marguerites, and kissed him with fresh and ruddy lips.

So then, when Patrasche arose, himself again, strong, big, gaunt, powerful, his great wistful eyes had a gentle astonishment in them that there were no curses to rouse him and no blows to drive him; and his heart awakened to a mighty love, which never wavered once in its fidelity whilst life abode with him.

But Patrasche, being a dog, was grateful. Patrasche lay pondering long with grave, tender, musing brown eyes, watching the movements of his friends.

Now, the old soldier, Jehan Daas, could do nothing for his living but limp about a little with a small cart, with which he carried daily the milk-cans of those happier neighbors who owned cattle away into the town of Antwerp. The villagers gave him the employment a little out of charity—more because it suited them well to send their milk into the town by so honest a carrier, and bide at home themselves to look after their gardens, their cows, their poultry, or their little fields. But it was becoming hard work for the old man. He was eighty-three, and Antwerp was a good league off, or more.

Patrasche watched the milk-cans come and go that one day when he had got well and was lying in the sun with the wreath of marguerites round his tawny neck.

The next morning, Patrasche, before the old man had touched the cart, arose and walked to it and placed himself betwixt its handles, and testified, as plainly as dumb show could do his desire and his ability to work in return for the bread of charity that he had eaten. Jehan Daas resisted long, for the old man was one of those who thought it a foul shame to bind dogs to labor for which Nature never formed them. But Patrasche would not be gainsaid: finding they did not harness him, he tried to draw the cart onward with his teeth.

At length Jehan Daas gave way, vanquished by the persistence and the gratitude of this creature whom he had succoured. He fashioned his cart so that Patrasche could run in it, and this he did every morning of his life thenceforward.

When the winter came. Jehan Daas thanked the blessed fortune that had brought him to the dying dog in the ditch that fair day of Louvain; for he was very old, and he grew feebler with each year, and he would ill have known how to pull his load of milk-cans over the snows and through the deep ruts in the mud if it had not been for the strength and the industry of the animal hehad befriended.

As for Patrasche, it seemed heaven to him. After the frightful burdens that his old master had compelled him to strain under, at the call of the whip at every step, it seemed nothing to him but amusement to step out with this little light green cart, with its bright brass cans, by the side of the gentle old man who always paid him with a tender caress and with a kindly word. Besides, his work was over by three or four in the day; and after that time he was free to do as he would to stretch himself, to sleep in the sun, to wander in the fields, to romp with the young child, or to play with his fellow-dogs. Patrasche was very happy.

Fortunately for his peace, his former owner was killed in a drunken brawl at the kermesse of Mechlin, and so sought not after him nor disturbed him in his new and well-loved home.

Chapter IV

A few years later, old Jehan Daas, who had always been a cripple, became so paralyzed with rheumatism that it was impossible for him to go out with the cart any more. Then little Nello, being now grown to his sixth year of age, and knowing the town well from having accompanied his grandfather so many times, took his place beside the cart, and sold the milk and received the coins in exchange, and brought them back to their respective owners with a pretty grace and seriousness which charmed all who beheld him.

The little Ardennois was a beautiful child,

with dark, grave, tender eyes, and a lovely bloom upon his face, and fair locks that clustered to his throat; and many an artist sketched the group as it went by him—the green cart with the brass flagons of Teniers and Mieris and Van Tal, and the great tawny-coloured, massive dog, with his belled harness that chimed cheerily as he went, and the small figure that ran beside him, which had little white feet in great wooden shoes, and a soft, grave, innocent, happy face like the little fair children of Rubens.

Nello and Patrasche did the work so well and so joyfully together that Jehan Daas himself, when the summer came and he was better again, had no need to stir out, but could sit in the door way in the sun and see them go forth through the garden wicket, and then doze and dream and pray a little, and then awake again as the clock tolled three and watch for their return. And on their return Patrasche would shake himself free of his harness with a bay of glee, and Nello would recount with pride the doings of the day; and they would all go in together to their meal of rye bread and milk or soup, and would see the shadows lengthen over the great plain, and see the twilight veil the fair cathedral spire; and then lie down together to sleep peacefully while the old man said a prayer.

So the days and the years went on, and the lives of Nello and Patrasche were happy, innocent, and healthful.

In the spring and summer especially were they glad. Flanders is not a lovely land, and around the burgh of Rubens it is perhaps least lovely of all.

Corn and colza, pasture and plough, succeed each other on the characterless plain in wearying repetition, and save by some gaunt gray tower, with its peal of pathetic bells, or some figure coming athwart the fields, made picturesque by a gleaner's bundle or a woodman's fagot, there is no change, no variety, no beauty anywhere; and he who has dwelt upon the mountains or amidst the forests feels oppressed as by imprisonment with the tedium and the endlessness of that vast and dreary level.

But it is green and very fertile, and it has wide horizons that have a certain charm of their own even in their dulness and monotony; and among the rushes by the water side the flowers grow, and the trees rise tall and fresh where the barges glide with their great hulks black against the sun, and their little green barrels and varicolored flags gay against the leaves.

Anyway, there is greenery and breadth of space enough to be as good as beauty to a child and a dog; and these two asked no better, when their work was done, than to lie buried in the lush grasses on the side of the canal, and watch the cumbrous vessels drifting by and bring the crisp salt smell of the sea among the blossoming scents of the country summer.

True, in the winter it was harder, and they had to rise in the darkness and the bitter cold, and they had seldom as much as they could have eaten any day, and the hut was scarce better than a shed when the nights were cold, although it looked so pretty in warm weather, buried in a great kindly-clambering vine, that never bore fruit, indeed, but which covered it with luxuriant green tracery all through the months of blossom and harvest. In winter the winds found many holes in the walls of the poor little hut, and the vine was black and leafless, and the bare lands looked very bleak and drear without, and sometimes within the floor was flooded and then frozen. In winter it was hard, and the snow numbed the little white limbs of Nello, and the icicles cut the brave, untiring feet of Patrasche.

But even then they were never heard to lament, either of them. The child's wooden shoes and the dog's four legs would trot manfully together over the frozen fields to the chime of the bells on the harness; and then sometimes, in the streets of Antwerp, some housewife would bring them a bowl of soup and a handful of bread, or some kindly trader would throw some billets of fuel into the little cart as it went homeward, or some woman in their own village would bid them keep a share of the milk they carried for their own food; and they would run over the white lands, through the early darkness, bright and happy, and burst with a shout of joy into their home.

So, on the whole, it was well with them, very well; and Patrasche, meeting on the highway or in the public streets the many dogs who toiled from daybreak into nightfall, paid only with blows and curses, and loosened from the shafts with a kick to starve and freeze as best they might—Patrasche in his heart was very grateful to his fate, and thought it the fairest and the kindliest the world could hold. Though he was often very hungry indeed when he lay down at night; though he had to work in the heats of summer noons and the rasping chills of winter dawns; though his feet were often tender with wounds from the sharp edges of the jagged pavement; though he had to perform tasks beyond his strength and against his nature—yet he was grateful and content: he did his duty with each day, and the eyes that he loved smiled down on him. It was sufficient for Patrasche.

Chapter V

There was only one thing which caused Patrasche any uneasiness in his life, and it was this. Antwerp, as all the world knows, is full at every turn of old piles of stones, dark and ancient, and majestic, standing in crooked courts, jammed against gateways and taverns, rising by the water's edge, with bells ringing above them in the air, and ever and again out of their arched doors a swell of music pealing.

There they remain, the grand old sanctuaries of the past, shut in amidst the squalor, the hurry, the crowds, the unloveliness, and the commerce of the modern world, and all day long the clouds drift and the birds circle and the winds sigh around them, and beneath the earth at their feet there sleeps— RUBENS.

And the greatness of the mighty master still rests upon Antwerp, and wherever we turn in its narrow streets his glory lies therein, so that all mean things are thereby transfigured; and as we pace slowly through the winding ways, and by the edge of the stagnant water, and through the noisome courts, his spirit abides with us, and the heroic beauty of his visions is about us, and the stones that once felt his footsteps and bore his shadow seem to arise and speak of him with living voices. For the city which is the tomb of Rubens still lives to us through him, and him alone.

Without Rubens, what were Antwerp? A dirty, dusky, bustling mart, which no man would ever care to look upon save the traders who do business on its wharves. With Rubens, to the whole world of men it is a sacred name, a sacred soil, a Bethlehem, where a god of Art saw light, a Golgotha, where a god of Art lies dead.

It is so quiet there by that great white sepulchre—so quiet, save only when the organ peals and, the choir cries aloud *the Salve Regina* or *the Kyrie Eleison*. Sure no artist ever had a greater grave stone than that pure marble sanctuary gives to him in the heart of his birthplace in the chancel of St. Jacques.

O nations! closely should you treasure your great men, for by them alone will the future know of you. Flanders in her generations has been wise. In his life she glorified this greatest of hersons, and in his death she magnifies his name. But her wisdom is very rare.

Now, the trouble of Patrasche was this. Into these great, sad piles of stones, that reared their melancholy majesty above the crowded roofs, the child Nello would many and many a time enter, and disappear through their dark arched portals, whilst Patrasche, left without upon the pavement, would wearily and vainly ponder on what could be the charm which thus allured from him his in separable and beloved companion. Once or twice he did essay to see for himself, clattering up the steps with his milk-cart behind him; but thereon he had been always sent back again summarily by a tall custodian in black clothes and silver chains of office; and fearful of bringing his little master into trouble, he desisted, and remained couched patiently before the churches until such time as the boy reappeared.

It was not the fact of his going into them which disturbed Patrasche: he knew that people went to church: all the village went to the small, tumble down, gray pile opposite the red windmill. What troubled him was that little Nello always looked strangely when he came out, always very flushed or very pale; and whenever he returned home after such visitations would sit silent and dreaming, not caring to play, but gazing out at the evening skies beyond the line of the canal, very subdued and almost sad.

"What was it?"wondered Patrasche. He thought it could not be good or natural for the little lad to be so grave, and in his dumb fashion he tried all he could to keep Nello by him in the sunny fields or in the busy marketplace. But to the churches Nello would go: most often of all would he go to the great cathedral; and Patrasche, left without on the stones by the iron fragments of Quentin Matsys's gate, would stretch himself and yawn and sigh, and even howl now and then, all in vain, until the doors closed and the child perforce came forth again, and winding his arms about the dog's neck would kiss him on his broad, tawney-colored forehead, and murmur always the same words: "If I could only see them, Patrasche! —if I could only see them!"

"What were they?"pondered Patrasche, looking up with large, wistful, sympathetic eyes.

One day, when the custodian was out of the way and the doors left ajar, he got in for a moment after his little friend and saw. "They"were two great covered pictures on either side of thechoir.

Nello was kneeling, rapt as in an ecstasy, before the altar-picture of *the Assumption*, and when he noticed Patrasche, and rose and drew the dog gently out into the air, his face was wet with tears, and he looked up at the veiled places as he passed them, and murmured to his companion, "It is so terrible not to see them, Patrasche, just because one is poor and cannot pay! He never meant that the poor should not see them when he painted them, I am sure. He would have had us see them any day, every day: that I am sure. And they keep them shrouded there—shrouded in the dark, the beautiful things! And they never feel the light, and no eyes look on them, unless rich people come and pay. If I could only see them, I would be content to die. "

But he could not see them, and Patrasche could not help him, for to gain the silver piece that the church exacts as the price for looking on the glories of *the Elevation of the Cross* and *the Descent of the Cross* was a thing as utterly beyond the powers of either of them as it would have been to scale the heights of the cathedral spire. They had never so much as a sou to spare: if they cleared enough to get a little wood for the stove, a little broth for the pot, it was the utmost they could do. And yet the heart of the child was set in sore and endless longing upon beholding the greatness of the two veiled Rubens.

Chapter VI

The whole soul of the little Ardennois thrilled and stirred with an absorbing passion for art. Going on his ways through the old city in the early days before the sun or the people had risen, Nello, who looked only a little peasant-boy, with a great dog drawing milk to sell from door to door, was in a heaven of dreams whereof Rubens was the god. Nello, cold and hungry, with stockingless feet in wooden shoes, and the winter winds blowing among his curls and lifting his poor thin garments, was in a rapture of meditation, wherein all that he saw was the beautiful fair face of the Mary of *the Assump-*

tion, with the waves of her golden hair lying upon her shoulders, and the light of an eternal sun shining down upon her brow. Nello, reared in poverty, and buffeted by fortune, and untaught in letters, and unheeded by men, had the compensation or the curse which is called Genius.

No one knew it. He as little as any. No one knew it. Only indeed Patrasche, who, being with him always, saw him draw with chalk upon the stones any and every thing that grew or breathed, heard him on his little bed of hay murmur all manner of timid, pathetic prayers to the spirit of the great master; watched his gaze darken and his face radiate at the evening glow of sunset or the rosy rising of the dawn; and felt many and many a time the tears of a strange, nameless pain and joy, mingled together, fall hotly from the bright young eyes upon his own wrinkled yellow forehead.

"I should go to my grave quite content if I thought, Nello, that when thou growest a man thou couldst own this hut and the little plot of ground, and labour for thyself, and be called Baas bythy neighbors, "said the old man Jehan many an hour from his bed. For to own a bit of soil, and to be called Baas—master—by the hamlet round, is to have achieved the highest ideal of a Flemish peasant; and the old soldier, who had wandered over all the earth in his youth, and had brought nothing back, deemed in his old age that to live and die on one spot in contented humility was the fairest fate he could desire for his darling. But Nello said nothing.

The same leaven was working in him that in other times begat Rubens and Jordaens and the Van Eycks, and all their wondrous tribe, and in times more recent begat in the green country of the Ardennes, where the Meuse washes the old walls of Dijon, the great artist of the Patroclus, whose genius is too near us for us aright to measure its divinity.

Nello dreamed of other things in the future than of tilling the little rood of earth, and living under the wattle roof, and being called Baas by neighbors a little poorer or a little less poor than himself. The cathedral spire, where it rose beyond the fields in the ruddy evening skies or in the dim, gray, misty mornings, said other things to him than this. But these he told only to Patrasche, whispering, childlike, his fancies in the dog's ear when they went together at their work through the fogs of the daybreak, or lay together at their rest among the rustling rushes by the water's side.

For such dreams are not easily shaped into speech to awake the slow sympathies of human auditors; and they would only have sorely perplexed and troubled the poor old man bedridden in his corner, who, for his part, whenever he had trodden the streets of Antwerp, had thought the daub of blue and red that they called a Madonna, on the walls of the wine-shop where he drank his sou's worth of black beer, quite as good as any of the famous altar pieces for which the stranger folk traveled far and wide into Flanders from every land on which the good sun shone.

There was only one other beside Patrasche to whom Nello could talk at all of his daring fantasies. This other was little Alois, who lived at the old red mill on the grassy mound, and whose father, the miller, was the best-to-do husbandmam in all the village. Little Alois was only a pretty baby with soft round, rosy features, made lovely by those sweet dark eyes that the Spanish rule has left in so many a Flemish face, in testimony of the Alvan dominion, as Spanish art has left broadsown throughout the country majestic palaces and stately courts, gilded house-fronts and Sculptured lintels-histories in blazonry and poems in stone.

Little Alois was often with Nello and Patrasche. They played in the fields, they ran in the snow, they gathered the daisies and bilberries, they went up to the old gray church together, and they often sat together by the broad wood-fire in the millhouse. Little Alois, indeed, was the richest child in the hamlet. She had neither brother nor sister; her blue serge dress had never a hole in it; at kermesse she had as many gilded nuts and Agni Dei in sugar as her hands could hold; and when she went up for her furst communion, her flaxen curls were covered with a cap of richest Mechlin lace, which had been her mother's and her grandmother's before it came to her. Men spoke already, though she had but twelve years, of the, good wife she would be for their sons to woo and win; but she herself was a little gay, simple child, in nowise conscious of her heritage, and she loved no playfellows so well as Jehan Daas's grandson, and his dog.

Chapter VII

One day her father, Baas Cogez, a good man, but somewhat stern, came on a pretty group in the long meadow behind the mill, where the aftermath had that day been cut. It was his little daughter sitting amidst the hay, with the great tawny head of Patrasche on her lap, and many wreaths of poppies and blue cornflowers round them both: on a clean smooth slab of pine wood the boy Nello drew their likeness with a stick of charcoal.

The miller stood and looked at the portrait with tears in his eyes, it was so strangely like, and he loved his only child closely and well. Then he roughly chid the little girl for idling there whilst her mother needed her within, and sent her indoors crying and afraid; then, turning, he snatched the wood from Nello's hands. "Dost do much of such folly? "he asked, but there was a tremble in his voice.

Nello coloured and hung his head. "I draw everything I see, "he murmured.

The miller was silent: then he stretched his hand out with a franc in it. "It is folly, as I say, and evil waste of time: nevertheless, it is like Alois, and will please the house-mother. Take this silver bit for it and leave it for me. "

The colour died out of the face of the young Ardennois; he lifted his head and put his hands behind his back. "Keep your money and the portrait both, Baas Cogez, "he said, simply. "You have been often good to me. "Then he called Patrasche to him, and walked away across the field.

"I could have seen them with that franc, "he murmured to Patrasche, "but I could not sell her picture—not even for them. "

Baas Cogez went into his millhouse sore troubled in his mind. "That lad must not be so much with Alois, "he said to his wife that night. "Trouble may come of it hereafter: he is fifteen now, and she is twelve; and the boy is comely of face and form. "

"And he is a good lad and a loyal, "said the housewife, feasting her eyes on the piece of pine wood where it was throned above the chimney with a cuckoo clock in oak and a Calvary in wax.

"Yea, I do not gainsay that, "said the miller, draining his pewter flagon.

"Then, if what you think of were ever to come to pass, "said the wife, hesitatingly, "would it matter so much? She will have enough for both, and one cannot be better than happy. "

"You are a woman, and therefore a fool, "said the miller, harshly, striking his pipe on the table. "The lad is naught but a beggar, and, with these painter's fancies, worse than a beggar. Have a care that they are not together in the future, or I will send the child to the surer keeping of the nuns of the Sacred Heart."

The poor mother was terrified, and promised humbly to do his will. Not that she could bring herself altogether to separate the child from her favorite playmate, nor did the miller even desire that extreme of cruelty to a young lad who was guilty of nothing except poverty. But there were many ways in which little Alois was kept away from her chosen companion; and Nello, being a boy proud and quiet and sensitive, was quickly wounded, and ceased to turn his own steps and those of Patrasche, as he had been used to do with every moment of leisure, to the old red millupon the slope.

What his offence was he did not know: he supposed he had in some manner angered Baas Cogez by taking the portrait of Alois in the meadow; and when the child who loved him would run to him and nestle her hand in his, he would smile at her very sadly and say with a tender concern for her before himself, "Nay, Alois, do not anger your father. He thinks that I make you idle, dear, and he is not pleased that you should be with me. He is a good man and loves you well: we will not anger him, Alois. "

But it was with a sad heart that he said it, and the earth did not look so bright to him as it had used to do when he went out at sunrise under the poplars down the straight roads with Patrasche. The old red mill had been a landmark to him, and he had been used to pause by it, going and coming, for a cheery greeting with its people as her little flaxen head rose above the low mill-wicket, and her little rosy hands had held out a bone or a crust to Patrasche.

Now the dog looked wistfully at a closed door, and the boy went on without pausing, with a pang at his heart, and the child sat within with tears dropping slowly on the knitting to which she was set on her little stool by the stove; and Baas Cogez, working among his sacks and his mill-gear, would harden his will, and say to himself, "It is best so. The lad is all but a beggar, and full of idle, dreaming fooleries. Who knows what mischief might not come of it in the future?"

So he was wise in his generation, and would not have the door unbarred, except upon rare and formal occasion, which seemed to have neither warmth nor mirth in them to the two children, who had been accustomed so long to a daily gleeful, careless, happy interchange of greeting, speech, and pastime, with no other watcher of their sports or auditor of their fancies than Patrasche, sagely shaking the brazen bells of his collar and responding with all a dog's swift sympathies to their every change of mood.

All this while the little panel of pine wood remained over the chimney in the mill-kitchen with the cuckoo clock and the waxen Calvary, and sometimes it seemed to Nello a little hard that whilst his gift was accepted he himself should be denied.

Chapter VIII

But he did not complain: it was his habit to be quiet: old Jehan Daas had said ever to him, "We are poor: we must take what God sends—the ill with the good: the poor cannot choose. "

To which the boy had always listened in silence, being reverent of his old grandfather; but nevertheless a certain vague, sweet hope, such as beguiles the children of genius, had whispered in his heart, "Yet the poor do choose sometimes—choose to be great, so that men cannot say them nay. "And he thought so still in his innocence; and one day, when the little Alois, finding him by chance alone among the cornfields by the canal, ran to him and held him close, and sobbed piteously because the morrow would be her saint's day, and for the first time in all her life her parents had failed to bid him to the little supper and romp in the great barns with which her feast-day was always celebrated, Nello had kissed her and murmured to her in firm faith, "It shall be different one day, Alois. One day that little bit of pine wood that your father has of mine shall be worth its weight in silver; and he will not shut the door against me then. Only love me always, dear little Alois, only love me always, and I will be great."

"And if I do not love you?" the pretty child asked, pouting a little through her tears, and moved by the instinctive coquetries of her sex.

Nello's eyes left her face and wandered to the distance, where in the red and gold of the Flemish night the cathedral spire rose. There was a smile on his face so sweet and yet so sad that little Alois was awed by it. "I will be great still," he said under his breath—"great still, or die, Alois."

"You do not love me," said the little spoilt child, pushing him away; but the boy shook his head and smiled, and went on his way through the tall yellow corn, seeing as in a vision some day in a fair future when he should come into that old familiar land and ask Alois of her people, and be not refused or denied, but received in honour, whilst the village folk should throng to look upon him and say in one another's ears, "Dost see him? He is a king among men, for he is a great artist and the world speaks his name; and yet he was only our poor little Nello, who was a beggar as one may say, and only got his bread by the help of his dog." And he thought how he would fold his grandsire in furs and purples, and portray him as the old man is portrayed in the Family in the chapel of St. Jacques; and of how he would hang the throat of Patrasche with a collar of gold, and place him on his right hand, and say to the people, "This was once my only friend;" and of how he would build himself a great white marble palace, and make to himself luxuriant gardens of pleasure, on the slope looking outward to where the cathedral spire rose, and not dwell in it himself; but summon to it, as to a home, all men young and poor and friendless, but of the will to do mighty things; and of how he would say to them always, if they sought to bless his name, "Nay, do not thank me—thank Rubens. Without him, what should I have been? "And these dreams, beautiful, impossible, innocent, free of all selfishness, full of heroical worship, were so closely about him as he went that he was happy—happy even on this sad anniversary of Alois's saint's day, when he and Patrasche went home by themselves to the little dark hut and the meal of black bread, whilst in the millhouse all the children of the village sang and laughed, and ate the big round cakes of Dijon and the almond gingerbread of Brabant, and danced in the great barn to the light of the stars and the music of flute and fiddle.

"Never mind, Patrasche, "he said, with his arms round the dog's neck as they both sat in the door of the hut, where the sounds of the mirth at the mill came down to them on the night air—"never mind. It shall all be changed by and by."

He believed in the future: Patrasche, of more experience and of more philosophy, thought that the loss of the mill supper in the present was ill compensated by dreams of milk and honey in some vague hereafter. And Patrasche growled whenever he passed by Baas Cogez.

"This is Alois's name-day, is it not?" said the old man Daas that night from the corner where he was stretched upon his bed of sacking.

The boy gave a gesture of assent: he wished that the old man's memory had erred a little, instead of keeping such sure account.

"And why not there?" his grandfather pursued. "Thou hast never missed a year before, Nello."

"Thou art too sick to leave," murmured the lad, bending his handsome head over the bed.

"Tut! Tut! Mother Nulette would have come and sat with me, as she does scores of times. What is the cause, Nello?"the old man persisted. "Thou surely hast not had ill words with thelittle one?"

"Nay; grandfather—never,"said the boy quickly, with a hot colour in his bent face. "Simply and truly, Baas Cogez did not have me asked this year. He has taken some whim against me."

"But thou hast done nothing wrong?"

"That I know—nothing. I took the portrait of Alois on a piece of pine: that is all."

"Ah!"The old man was silent: the truth suggested itself to him with the boy's innocent answer. He was tied to a bed of dried leaves in the corner of a wattle hut, but he had not wholly forgotten what the ways of the world were like.

He drew Nello's fair head fondly to his breast with a tenderer gesture. "Thou art very poor, my child,"he said with a quiver the more in his aged, trembling voice—"so poor! It is very hard for thee."

"Nay, I am rich,"murmured Nello; and in his innocence he thought so—rich with the imperishable powers that are mightier than the might of kings. And he went and stood by the door of the hut in the quiet autumn night, and watched the stars troop by and the tall poplars bend and shiver in the wind. All the casements of the millhouse were lighted, and every now and then the notes of the flute came to him. The tears fell down his cheeks, for he was but a child, yet he smiled, for he said to himself, "In the future! "

He stayed there until all was quite still and dark, then he and Patrasche went within and slept together, long and deeply, side by side.

Chapter IX

Now he had a secret which only Patrasche knew.

There was a little outhouse to the hut, which no one entered but himself—a dreary place, but with abundant clear light from the north. Here he had fashioned himself rudely an easel in rough lumber, and here on a great gray sea of stretched paper he had given shape to one of the innumerable fancies which possessed his brain. No one had ever taught him anything; colours he had no means to buy; he had gone without bread many a time to procure even the few rude vehicles that he had here; and it was only in black or white that he could fashion the things he saw. This great figure which he had drawn here in chalk was only an old man sitting on a fallen tree—only that. He had seen old Michel the woodman sitting so at evening many a time. He had never had a soul to tell him of outline or perspective, of anatomy or of shadow, and yet he had given all the weary, worn-out age, all the sad, quiet patience, all the rugged, careworn pathos of his original, and given them so that the old lonely figure was a poem, sitting there, meditative and alone, on the dead tree, with the darkness of the descending night behind him.

It was rude, of course, in a way, and had many faults, no doubt; and yet it was real, true in Nature true in art, and very mournful, and in a manner beautiful.

Patrasche had lain quiet countless hours watching its gradual creation after the labour of each day was done, and he knew that Nello had a hope— vain and wild perhaps, but strongly chefisbed—of sending this great drawing to compete for a prize of two hundred francs a year which it was announced in Antwerp would be open to every lad of talent, scholar or peasant, under eighteen, who would attempt to win it with some unaided work of chalk or pencil. Three of the foremost artists in the town of Rubens were to be the judges and elect the victor according to his merits.

All the spring and summer and autumn Nello had been at work upon this treasure, which, if triumphant, would build him his first step toward independence and the mysteries of the art which he blindly, ignorantly, and yet passionately adored.

He said nothing to any one: his grandfather would not have understood, and little Alois was lost to him. Only to Patrasche he told all, and whispered, "Rubens would give it me, I think, if he knew. "

Patrasche thought so too, for he knew that Rubens had loved dogs or he had never painted them with such exquisite fidelity; and men who loved dogs were, as Patrasche knew, always pitiful.

The drawings were to go in on the first day of December, and the decision be given on the twenty-fourth, so that he who should win might rejoice with all his people at the Christmas season.

In the twilight of a bitter wintry day, and with a beating heart, now quick with hope, now faint with fear, Nello placed the great picture on his little green milk-cart, and took it, with the help of Patrasche, into the town, and there left it, as enjoined, at the doors of a public building.

"Perhaps it is worth nothing at all. How can I tell?"he thought, with the heart sickness of a great timidity. Now that he had left it there, it seemed to him so hazardous, so vain, so foolish, to dream that he, a little lad with bare feet, who barely knew his letters, could do anything at which great painters, real artists, could ever deign to look. Yet he took heart as he went by the cathedral: the lordly form of Rubens seemed to rise from the fog and the darkness, and to loom in its magnificence before him, whilst the lips, with their kindly smile, seemed to him to murmur, "Nay, have courage! It was not by a weak heart and by faint fears that I wrote my name for all time upon Antwerp. "

Nello ran home through the cold night, comforted. He had done his best: the rest must be as God willed, he thought, in that innocent, unquestioning faith which had been taught him in thelittle gray chapel among the willows and the poplar-trees.

Chapter X

The winter was very sharp already. That night, after they reached the hut, snow fell; and fell for very many days after that, so that the paths and the divisions in the fields were all obliterated, and all the smaller streams were frozen over, and the cold was intense upon the plains. Then, indeed, it became hard work to go round for the milk while the world was all dark, and carry it through the darkness to the silent town. Hard work, especially for Patrasche, for the passage of the years, that were only bringing Nello a stronger youth, were bringing him old age, and his joints were stiff and his bones ached often. But he would never give up his share of the labour. Nello would fain have spared him and drawn the cart himself, but Patrasche would not allow it. All he would ever permit or accept was the help of a thrust from behind to the truck as it lumbered along through the ice-ruts. Patrasche had lived in harness, and he was proud of it. He suffered a great deal sometimes from frost, and the terrible roads, and the rheumatic pains of his limbs, but he only drew his breath hard and bent his stout neck, and trod onward with steady patience.

"Rest thee at home, Patrasche—it is time thou didst rest—and I can quite well push in the cart by myself, "urged Nello many a morning; but Patrasche, who understood him aright, would no more have consented to stay at home than a veteran soldier to shirk when the charge was sounding; and every day he would rise and place himself in his shafts, and plod along over the snow through the fields that his four round feet had left their print upon so many, many years.

"One must never rest till one dies, "thought Patrasche; and sometimes it seemed to him that that time of rest for him was not very far off. His sight was less clear than it had been, and it gave him pain to rise after the night's sleep, though he would never lie a moment in his straw when once the bell of the chapel tolling five let him know that the daybreak of labor had begun.

"My poor Patrasche, we shall soon lie quiet together, you and I, "said old Jehan Daas, stretching out to stroke the head of Patrasche with the old withered hand which had always sharedwith him its one poor crust of bread; and the hearts of the old man and the old dog ached together with one thought: When they were gone, who would care for their darling?

One afternoon, as they came back from Antwerp over the snow, which had become hard and smooth as marble over all the Flemish plains, they found dropped in the road a pretty little puppet, a tambourine-player, all scarlet and gold, about six inches high, and, unlike greater personages when Fortune lets them drop, quite unspoiled and unhurt by its fall. It was a pretty toy. Nello tried to find its owner, and, failing, thought that it was just the thing to please Alois.

It was quite night when he passed the millhouse: he knew the little window of her room. It could be no harm, be thought, if he gave her his little piece of treasure trove, they had been play-fellows so long. There was a shed with a sloping roof beneath her casement: he climbed it and tapped softly at the lattice: there was a little light within. The child opened it and looked out half frightened.

Nello put the tambourine-player into her hands. "Here is a doll I found in the snow, Alois. Take it, "he whispered—"take it, and God bless thee, dear! "

He slid down from the shed-roof before she had time to thank him, and ran off through the darkness.

That night there was a fire at the mill. Outbuildings and much corn were destroyed, although the mill itself and the dwelling-house were unharmed. All the village was out in terror, and engines came tearing through the snow from Antwerp. The miller was insured, and would lose nothing: nevertheless, he was in furious wrath, and declared aloud that the fire was due to no accident, but to some foul intent.

Nello, awakened from his sleep, ran to help with the rest: Baas Cogez thrust him angrily aside. "Thou wert loitering here after dark," he said roughly. "I believe, on my soul, that thou dost know more of the fire than any one."

Nello heard him in silence, stupefied, not supposing that any one could say such things except in jest, and not comprehending how any one could pass a jest at such a time.

Nevertheless, the miller said the brutal thing openly to many of his neighbours in the day that followed; and though no serious charge was ever preferred against the lad, it got bruited about that

Nello had been seen in the mill-yard after dark on some unspoken errand, and that he bore Baas Cogez a grudge for forbidding his intercourse with little Alois; and so the hamlet, which followed the sayings of its richest landowner servilely, and whose families all hoped to secure the riches of Alois in some future time for their sons, took the hint to give grave looks and cold words to old Jehan Daas's grandson.

No one said anything to him openly, but all the village agreed together to humor the miller's prejudice, and at the cottages and farms where Nello and Patrasche called every morning for the milk for Antwerp, downcast glances and brief phrases replaced to them the broad smiles and cheerful greetings to which they had been always used. No one really credited the miller's absurd suspicion, nor the outrageous accusations born of them, but the people were all very poor and very ignorant, and the one rich man of the place had pronounced against him. Nello, in his innocence and his friendlessness, had no strength to stem the popular tide.

"Thou art very cruel to the lad, "the miller's wife dared to say, weeping, to her lord. "Sure he is an innocent lad and a faithful, and would never dream of any such wickedness, however sore his heart might be. "

But Baas Cogez being an obstinate man, having once said a thing held to it doggedly, though in his innermost soul he knew well the injustice that he was committing.

Meanwhile, Nello endured the injury done against him with a certain proud patience that disdained to complain: he only gave way a little when he was quite alone with old Patrasche. Besides, he thought, "If my picture should win! They will be sorry then, perhaps. "

Still, to a boy not quite sixteen, and who had dwelt in one little world all his short life, and in his childhood had been caressed and applauded on all sides, it was a hard trial to have thewhole of that little world turn against him for naught. Especially hard in that bleak, snowbound, famine-stricken winter-time, when the only light and warmth there could be found abode beside the village hearths and in the kindly greetings of neighbours.

In the wintertime all drew nearer to each other, all to all, except to Nello and Patrasche, with whom none now would have anything to do, and who were left to fare as they might with the old paralyzed, bedridden man in the little cabin, whose fire was often low, and whose board was often without bread, for there was a buyer from Antwerp who had taken to drive his mule in of a day for the milk of the various dairies, and there were only three or four of the people who had refused his terms of purchase and remained faithful to the little green cart. So that the burden which Patrasche drew had become very light, and the centime-pieces in Nello's pouch had become, alas! Very small likewise.

The dog would stop, as usual, at all the familiar gates, which were now closed to him, and look up at them with wistful, mute appeal; and it cost the neighbours a pang to shut their doors and their hearts, and let Patrasche draw his cart on again, empty. Nevertheless, they did it, for they desired to please Baas Cogez.

Chapter XI

Noel was close at hand.

The weather was very wild and cold. The snow was six feet deep, and the ice was firm enough to bear oxen and men upon it everywhere. At this season the little village was always gay andcheerful. At the poorest dwelling there were possets and cakes, joking and dancing, sugared saints and gilded Jesus. The merry Flemish bells jingled everywhere on the horses; everywhere within doors some well-filled soup-pot sang and smoked over the stove; and everywhere over the snow without laughing maidens pattered in bright kerchiefs and stout kirtles, going to and from the mass. Only in the little hut it was very dark and very cold.

Nello and Patrasche were left utterly alone, for one night in the week before the Christmas Day, Death entered there, and took away from life forever old Jehan Daas, who had never known life aught save its poverty and its pains. He had long been half dead, incapable of any movement except a feeble gesture, and powerless for anything beyond a gentle word; and yet his loss fell on them both with a great horror in it: they mourned him passionately. He had passed away from them in his sleep, and when in the gray dawn they learned their bereavement, unutterable solitude and desolation seemed to close around them. He had long been only a poor, feeble, paralyzed old man, who could not raise a hand in their defence, but he had loved them well: his smile had always welcomed their return.

They mourned for him unceasingly, refusing to be comforted, as in the white winter day they followed the deal shell that held his body to the nameless grave by the little gray church. They were his only mourners, these two whom he had left friendless upon earth-the young boy and the old dog. "Surely, he will relent now and let the poor lad come hither? "thought the miller's wife, glancing at her husband smoking by the hearth.

Baas Cogez knew her thought, but he hardened his heart, and would not unbar his door as the little, humble funeral went by. "The boy is a beggar, "he said to himself: "he shall not be about Alois. "

The woman dared not say anything aloud, but when the grave was closed and the mourners had gone, she put a wreath of immortelles into Alois' hands and bade her go and lay it reverently on the dark, unmarked mound where the snow was displaced.

Nello and Patrasche went home with broken hearts. But even of that poor, melancholy, cheerless home they were denied the consolation. There was a month's rent overdue for their little home, and when Nello had paid the last sad service to the dead he had not a coin left. He went and begged grace of the owner of the hut, a cobbler who went every Sunday night to drink his pint of wine and smoke with Baas Cogez. The cobbler would grant no mercy. He was a harsh, miserly man, and loved money. He claimed in default of his rent every stick and stone, every pot and pan, in the hut, and bade Nello and Patrasche be out of it on the morrow.

Now, the cabin was lowly enough, and in some sense miserable enough, and yet their hearts clove to it with a great affection. They had been so happy there, and in the summer, with its clambering vine and its flowering beans, it was so pretty and bright in the midst of the sun-lighted fields! There life in it had been full of labour and privation, and yet they had been so well content, so gay of heart, running together to meet the old man's never-failing smile of welcome!

All night long the boy and the dog sat by the

fireless hearth in the darkness, drawn close together for warmth and sorrow. Their bodies were insensible to the cold, but their hearts seemed frozen in them.

When the morning broke over the white chill earth it was the morning of Christmas Eve. With a shudder Nello clasped close to him his only friend, while his tears fell hot and fast on the dog's frank forehead. "Let us go, Patrasche—dear, dear Patrasche, "he murmured. "We will not wait to be kicked out: let us go. "

Patrasche had no will but his, and they went sadly, side by side, out from the little place which was so dear to them both, and in which every humble, homely thing was to them precious and beloved. Patrasche drooped his head wearily as he passed by his own green cart: it was no longer his—it had to go with the rest to pay the rent, and his brass harness lay idle and glittering on the snow. The dog could have lain down beside it and died for very heartsickness as he went, but whilst the lad lived and needed him Patrasche would not yield and give way.

They took the old accustomed road into Antwerp. The day had yet scarce more than dawned, most of the shutters were still closed, but some of the villagers were about. They took no notie whilst the dog and the boy passed by them. At one door Nello paused and looked wistfully within: his grandfather had done many a kindly turn in neighbour's service to the people who dwelt there.

"Would you give Patrasche a crust? "he said, timidly. "He is old, and he has had nothing since last forenoon. "

The woman shut the door hastily, murmuring some vague saying about wheat and rye being very dear that season. The boy and the dog went on again wearily: they asked no more.

By slow and painful ways they reached Antwerp as the chimes tolled ten.

"If I had anything about me I could sell to get him bread! "thought Nello, but he had nothing except the wisp of linen and serge that covered him, and his pair of wooden shoes.

Patrasche understood, and nestled his nose into the lad's hand, as though to pray him not to be disquieted for any woe or want of his.

The winner of the drawing-prize was to be proclaimed at noon, and to the public building where he had left his treasure Nello made his way. On the steps and in the entrance-hall there was a crowd of youths—some of his age, some older, all with parents or relatives or friends. His heart was sick with fear as he went among them, holding Patrasche close to him. The great bells of the city clashed out the hour of noon with brazen clamor. The doors of the inner hall were opened; the eager, panting throng rushed in: it was known that the selected picture would be raised above the rest upon a wooden dais.

A mist obscured Nello's sight, his head swam, his limbs almost failed him. When his vision cleared he saw the drawing raised on high: it was not his own! A slow, sonorous voice was proclaiming aloud that victory had been adjudged to Stephen Kiesslinger, born in the burgh of Antwerp, son of a wharfinger in that town.

Chapter XII

When Nello recovered his consciousness he was lying on the stones without, and Patrasch was trying with every art he knew to call him back to life. In the distance a throng of the youths of Antwerp were shouting around their successful comrade, and escorting him with acclamations to his home upon the quay.

The boy staggered to his feet and drew the dog into his embrace. "It is all over, dear Patrasche, "he murmured—"all over! "

He rallied himself as best he could, for he was weak from fasting, and retraced his steps to the village. Patrasche paced by his side with his head drooping and his old limbs feeble fromhunger and sorrow.

The snow was falling fast: a keen hurricane blew from the north: it was bitter as death on the plains. It took them long to traverse the familiar path, and the bells were sounding four of the clock as they approached the hamlet. Suddenly Patrasche paused, arrested by a scent in the snow, scratched, whined, and drew out with his teeth a small case of brown leather. He held it up to Nello in the darkness. Where they were there stood a little Calvary, and a lamp burned dully under the cross: the boy mechanically turned the case to the light: on it was the name of Baas Cogez, and within it were notes for two thousand francs.

The sight roused the lad a little from his stupor. He thrust it in his shirt, and stroked Patrasche and drew him onward. The dog looked up wistfully in his face.

Nello made straight for the millhouse, and

went to the house-door and struck on its panels. The miller's wife opened it weeping, with little Alois clinging close to her skirts. "Is it thee, thou poor lad?" She said kindly through her tears. "Get thee gone ere the Baas see thee. We are in sore trouble tonight. He is out seeking for a power of money that he has let fall riding homeward, and in this snow he never will find it; and God knows it will go nigh to ruin us. It is Heaven's own judgment for the things we have done to thee."

Nello put the notecase in her hand and called Patrasche within the house. "Patrasche found the money tonight," he said quickly. "Tell Baas Cogez so: I think he will not deny the dog shelter and food in his old age. Keep him from pursuing me, and I pray of you to be good to him."

Ere either woman or dog knew what he meant he had stooped and kissed Patrasche: then closed the door hurriedly, and disappeared in the gloom of the fast-falling night.

The woman and the child stood speechless

with joy and fear: Patrasche vainly spent the fury of his anguish against the ironbound oak of the barred house-door. They did not dare unbar the door and let him forth: they tried all they could to solace him. They brought him sweet cakes and juicy meats; they tempted him with the best they had; they tried to lure him to abide by the warmth of the hearth; but it was of no avail. Patrasche refused to be comforted or to stir from the barred portal.

It was six o'clock when from an opposite entrance, the miller at last came, jaded and broken, into his wife's presence. "It is lost for ever, "he said, with an ashen cheek and a quiver in his stern voice. "We have looked with lanterns everywhere: it is gone—the little maiden's portion and all! "

His wife put the money into his hand, and told him how it had come to her. The strong man sank trembling into a seat and covered his face, ashamed and almost afraid. "I have been cruel to the lad, "he muttered at length: "I deserved not to have good at his hands. "

Little Alois, taking courage, crept close to her father and nestled against him her fair curly head. "Nello may come here again, father? "she whispered. "He may come tomorrow as heused to do? "

The miller pressed her in his arms: his hard, sunburned face was very pale and his mouth trembled. "Surely, surely, "he answered his child. "He shall bide here on Christmas Day, and any other day he will. God helping me, I will make amends to the boy—I will make amends. "

Little Alois kissed him in gratitude and joy, then slid from his knees and ran to where the dog kept watch by the door. "And tonight I may feast Patrasche? "she cried in a child's thoughness glee.

Her father bent his head gravely: "Ay, ay: let the dog have the best; "for the stern old man was moved and shaken to his heart's depths.

It was Christmas Eve, and the millhouse was filled with oak logs and squares of turf, with cream and honey, with meat and bread, and the rafters were hung with wreaths of evergreen, and the Calvary and the cuckoo clock looked out from a mass of holly. There were little paper lanterns, too, for Alois, and toys of various fashions and sweetmeats in bright-pictured papers. There were light and warmth and abundance everywhere, and the child would fain have made the dog a guest honored and feasted.

But Patrasche would neither lie in the warmth nor share in the cheer. Famished he was and very cold, but without Nello he would partake neither of comfort nor food. Against all temptation he was proof, and close against the door he leaned always, watching only for a means of escape.

"He wants the lad, "said Baas Cogez. "Good dog! Good dog! I will go over to the lad the first thing at day-dawn. "For no one but Patrasche knew that Nello had left the hut, and no one but Patrasche divined that Nello had gone to face starvation and misery alone.

Chapter XIII

The mill-kitchen was very warm: great logs crackled and flamed on the hearth; neighbors came in for a glass of wine and a slice of the fat goose baking for supper. Alois, gleeful and sure of her playmate back on the morrow, bounded and sang, and tossed back her yellow hair. Baas Cogez, in the fulness of his heart, smiled on her through moistened eyes, and spoke of the way in which he would befriend her favorite companion; the house-mother sat with calm, contented face at the spinning-wheel; the cuckoo in the clock chirped mirthful hours. Amidst it all Patrasche was bidden with a thousand words of welcome to tarry there a cherished guest. But neither peace nor plenty could allure him where Nello was not.

When the supper smoked on the board, and the voices were loudest and gladdest, and the Christ-child brought choicest gifts to Alois, Patrasche, watching always an occasion, glided out when the door was unlatched by a careless new comer, and as swiftly as his weak and tired limbs would bear him sped over the snow in the bitter, black night. He had only one thought-to follow Nello. A human friend might have paused for the pleasant meal, the cheery warmth, the cosy slumber; but that was not the friendship of Patrasche. He remembered a bygone time, when an old man and a little child had found him sick unto death in the wayside ditch.

Snow had fallen freshly all the evening long; it was now nearly ten; the trail of the boy's footsteps was almost obliterated. It took Patrasche long to discover any scent. When at last he found it, it was lost again quickly; and lost and recovered, and again lost and again recovered, a hundred times, or more.

The night was very wild. The lamps under the wayside crosses were blown out; the roads were sheets of ice; the impenetrable darkness hid every trace of habitations; there was no living thing abroad. All the cattle were housed, and in all the huts and homesteads men and women rejoiced and feasted. There was only Patrasche out in the cruel cold-old and famished and full of pain, but with the strength and the patience of a great love to sustain him in his search.

The trail of Nello's steps, faint and obscure as it was under the new snow, went straightly along the accustomed tracks into Antwerp.

It was past midnight when Patrasche traced it over the boundaries of the town and into the narrow, tortuous, gloomy streets. It was all quite dark in the town, save where some light gleamed ruddily through the crevices of house-shutters, or some group went homeward with lanterns chanting drinking-songs. The streets were all white with ice: the high walls and roofs loomed black against them. There was scarce a sound save the riot of the winds down the passages as they tossed the creaking signs and shook the tall lamp-irons.

So many passers by had trodden through and through the snow, so many diverse paths had crossed and recrossed each other, that the dog had a hard task to retain any hold on the track hefollowed. But he kept on his way, though the cold pierced him to the bone, and the jagged ice cut his feet, and the hunger in his body gnawed like a rat's teeth. He kept on his way, a poor gaunt, shivering thing, and by long patience traced the steps he loved into the very heart of the burgh and up to the steps of the great cathedral.

"He is gone to the things that he loved, "thought Patrasche: he could not understand, but he was full of sorrow and of pity for the art-passion that to him was so incomprehensible and yet so sacred.

The portals of the cathedral were unclosed after the midnight mass. Some heedlessness in the custodians, too eager to go home and feast or sleep, or too drowsy to know whether they turned the keys aright, had left one of the doors unlocked. By that accident the foot falls Patrasche sought had passed through into the building, leaving the white marks of snow upon the dark stone floor. By that slender white thread, frozen as it fell, he was guided through the intense silence, through the immensity of the vaulted space-guided straight to the gates of the chancel, and, stretched there upon the stones, he found Nello. He crept up, and touched the face of the boy. "Didst thou dream that I should be faithless and forsake thee? I a dog? "said that mute caress.

The lad raised himself with a low cry and clasped him close. "Let us lie down and die together, "he murmured. "Men have no need of us, and we are all alone. "

In answer, Patrasche crept closer yet, and laid his head upon the young boy's breast. The great tears stood in his brown, sad eyes: not for himself—for himself he was happy.

They lay close together in the piercing cold. The blasts that blew over the Flemish dikes from the northern seas were like waves of ice, which froze every living thing they touched. The interior of the immense vault of stone in which they were was even more bitterly chill than the snow-covered plains without. Now and then a bat moved in the shadows-now and then a gleam of light came on the ranks of carven figures. Under the Rubens they lay together, quite still, and soothed almost into a dreaming slumber by the numbing narcotic of the cold. Together they dreamed of the old glad days when they had chased each other through the flowering grasses of the summer meadows, or sat hidden in the tall bulrushes by the water's side, watching the boatsgo seaward in the sun.

No anger had ever separated them; no cloud had ever come between them; no roughness on the one side, no faithlessness on the other, had ever obscured their perfect love and trust. All through their short lives they had done their duty as it had come to them, and had been happy in the mere sense of living, and had begrudged nothing to any man or beast, and had been quite content because quite innocent. And in the faintness of famine and of the frozen blood that stole dully and slowly through their veins, it was of the days they had spent together that they dreamed, lying there in the long watches of the night of Noel.

Suddenly through the darkness a great white radiance streamed through the vastness of the aisles; the moon, that was at her height, had broken through the clouds, the snow had ceased to fall; the light reflected from the snow without was clear as the light of dawn. It fell through the arches full upon the two pictures above, from which the boy on his entrance had flung back theveil: *the Elevation* and *the Descent of the Cross* were for one instant visible.

Nello rose to his feet and stretched his arms to

them; the tears of a passionate ecstasy glistened on the paleness of his face. "I have seen them at last! "he cried aloud. "O God, it isenough! "

His limbs failed under him, and he sank upon his knees, still gazing upward at the majesty that he adored. For a few brief moments the light illumined the divine visions that had been denied to him so long-light clear and sweet and strong as though it streamed from the throne of Heaven. Then suddenly it passed away: once more a great darkness covered the face of Christ.

The arms of the boy drew close again the body of the dog. "We shall see His face—there, "he murmured, "and He will not part us, I think. "

Chapter XIV

ON the morrow, by the chancel of the cathedral, the people of Antwerp found them both. They were both dead: the cold of the night had frozen into stillness alike the young life and the old. When the Christmas morning broke and the priests came to the temple, they saw them lying thus on the stones together. Above the veils were drawn back from the great visions of Rubens, and the fresh rays of the sunrise touched the thorn crowned head of the Christ.

As the day grew on there came an old, hard-featured man who wept as women weep. "I was cruel to the lad, "he muttered, "and now I would have made amends—yea, to the half of my substance—and he should have been to me as a son. "

There came also, as the day grew apace, a painter who had fame in the world, and who was liberal of hand and of spirit. "I seek one who should have had the prize yesterday had worth won, "he said to the people"A boy of rare promise and genius. An old wood cutter on a fallen tree at eventide—that was all his theme. But there was greatness for the future in it. I would fain find him, and take him with me and teach him Art. "

And a little child with curling fair hair, sobbing bitterly as she clung to her father's arm, cried aloud, "Oh, Nello, come! We have all ready for thee. The Christ-child's hands are full of gifts, and the old piper will play for us; and the mother says thou shalt stay by the hearth and burn nuts with us all the Noel week long—yes, even to the Feast of the

Kings! And Patrasche will be so happy! Oh, Nello, wake and come! "

But the young pale face, turned upward to the light of the great Rubens with a smile upon its mouth, answered them all, "It is too late. "

For the sweet, sonorous bells went ringing through the frost, and the sunlight shone upon the plains of snow, and the populace trooped gay and glad through the streets, but Nello and Patrasche no more asked charity at their hands. All they needed now Antwerp gave unbidden.

Death had been more pitiful to them than longer life would have been. It had taken the one in the loyalty of love, and the other in the innocence of faith, from a world which for love has no recompense, and for faith no fulfilment.

All their lives they had been together, and in their deaths they were not divided: for when they were found the arms of the boy were folded too closely around the dog to be severed without violence, and the people of their little village, contrite and ashamed, implored a special grace for them, and, making them one grave, laid them to rest there side by side—forever.

图书在版编目 (CIP) 数据

佛兰德斯的狗 /（英）奥维达著；王家湘译. — 北京：北京十月文艺出版社，2025.4
ISBN 978-7-5302-2337-6

Ⅰ. ①佛… Ⅱ. ①奥… ②王… Ⅲ. ①儿童小说—中篇小说—英国—近代 Ⅳ. ① I561.84

中国国家版本馆 CIP 数据核字 (2023) 第 217220 号

佛兰德斯的狗
FOLANDESI DE GOU
（英）奥维达　著　王家湘　译

出　　版	北京出版集团
	北京十月文艺出版社
地　　址	北京北三环中路 6 号
邮　　编	100120
网　　址	www.bph.com.cn
发　　行	新经典发行有限公司
	电话 010-68423599
经　　销	新华书店
印　　刷	北京盛通印刷股份有限公司
版　　次	2025 年 4 月第 1 版
印　　次	2025 年 4 月第 1 次印刷
开　　本	850 毫米 ×1168 毫米 1/32
印　　张	5.75
字　　数	84 千字
书　　号	ISBN 978-7-5302-2337-6
定　　价	49.80 元

如有印装质量问题，由本社负责调换
质量监督电话　010-58572393

版权所有，未经书面许可，不得转载、复制、翻印，违者必究。